ENDING AND UNENDING AGONY

Sara Guyer and Brian McGrath, series editors

Lit Z embraces models of criticism uncontained by conventional notions of history, periodicity, and culture, and committed to the work of reading. Books in the series may seem untimely, anachronistic, or out of touch with contemporary trends because they have arrived too early or too late.

At least since Friedrich Schlegel, thinking that affirms literature's own untimeliness has been named romanticism. Recalling this history, Lit Z exemplifies the survival of romanticism as a mode of contemporary criticism, as well as forms of contemporary criticism that demonstrate the unfulfilled possibilities of romanticism. Whether or not they focus on the romantic period, books in this series epitomize romanticism as a way of thinking that compels another relation to the present.

Lit Z is the first book series to take seriously this capacious sense of romanticism. Its books explore the creative potential of reading's untimeliness and history's enigmatic force.

ENDING AND UNENDING AGONY

On Maurice Blanchot

Philippe Lacoue-Labarthe
translated by Hannes Opelz

Fordham University Press
New York 2015

This book was originally published in French as Philippe Lacoue-Labarthe, *Agonie terminée, agonie interminable sur Maurice Blanchot: Suivi de L'émoi* © Editions Galilée, 2011.

This work has been published with the assistance of the French Ministry of Culture—National Center for the Book.

Ouvrage publié avec le concours du Ministère français chargé de la culture—Centre National du Livre.

Fordham University Press also publishes its books in a variety of electronic formats. Some content that appears in print may not be available in electronic books.

Visit us online at www.fordhampress.com.

Library of Congress Control Number: 2015942655

Printed in the United States of America

17 16 15 5 4 3 2 1

First edition

Contents

Translator's Note

The present volume is a translation of Philippe Lacoue-Labarthe's *Agonie terminée, agonie interminable. Sur Maurice Blanchot* (Paris: Galilée, 2011), published posthumously and edited by Aristide Bianchi and Leonid Kharlamov. With the exception of "[In 1976, Malraux . . .]" and "Interview with Pascal Possoz," that French edition is thus the source text for the present translation. (Full bibliographical details on all texts translated here are provided in the Bibliographical Note at the end of this volume.) The present volume also includes a translation of the "Présentation" (here, the Introduction) by the editors of the original French text, which offers a thorough overview of the book's complicated genesis and introduces readers to the aesthetic, political, and ethical stakes of its engagement with its subject, Maurice Blanchot, quoting at length from a wide selection of previously unpublished material (conference papers, seminar notes, correspondence, radio broadcasts, etc.) drawn from the Philippe Lacoue-Labarthe archives at the Institut Mémoires de l'édition contemporaine (IMEC).

As indicated above, two texts translated for this volume do not appear in the French edition. The first, left untitled by its author (and retitled for the present translation), is a response to a survey on intellectuals carried out by the French journal *Lignes* and was originally published in October 1997 under the title (supplied by the journal) "Les intellectuels. Tentative de définition par eux-mêmes, enquête" (Intellectuals: An Attempt at Self-Definition—A Survey). Considering the central role played by Blanchot in this text, it seemed only fitting to include it here, all the more so because it brings into sharp focus the ethico-political dimension of Lacoue-Labarthe's engagement with Blanchot, which, while decisively at stake in other texts featured in the present volume, never enjoys the kind of direct attention it receives in the text in question.

The second text not appearing in the French edition is a two-part interview conducted by gastroenterologist Pascal Possoz in December 2001 and January 2002. At the time of the interview, Possoz was working on a doctoral dissertation in psychopathology that set out to formulate a clinical interpretation of a number of motifs found in Blanchot's work, among others that of the "primal scene." Given Lacoue-Labarthe's sustained dialogue with

Blanchot around the question of the primal scene, Possoz took the initiative in interviewing the former on the subject. The interview, which served as a kind of memorandum to assist Possoz in his doctoral work and was thus never intended for publication, was rediscovered in 2011, just as *Agonie terminée, agonie interminable* was going to press. In addition to shedding light on the metapsychological and psychoanalytical stakes of the dialogue between Lacoue-Labarthe and Blanchot, this heretofore unpublished interview also gives readers new historical and (auto)biographical insights into Lacoue-Labarthe's long-lasting conversation with Blanchot's oeuvre, not only as a thinker but also as a poet and an editor.

The two texts in question, then, together with "Dismay" (included in the French edition and discussed in the Introduction), make up the Appendix to this volume. To my knowledge, neither the texts in the Appendix nor those in the book proper have been translated into English, except for "Fidelities" and "The Contestation of Death," translated by Michael Syrotinski and Philip Anderson, respectively.[1] Although I have consulted their translations only after the fact (my reasoning being that translating a text that is part and parcel of a book is something quite different from translating what was at the time of its first publication a stand-alone piece), I have often gratefully relied upon them—at times following them closely, almost word for word. Nevertheless, beyond contextual differences, a number of discrepancies separate these translations from the (re)translations presented in this volume. Two, at least, are worth mentioning here. The first is empirical. The source texts used by Syrotinski and Anderson differ from the final versions published in *Agonie terminée, agonie interminable*, the latter being longer, sometimes only slightly (by one or two sentences), other times more significantly (one or two pages). The second discrepancy is theoretical. At crucial points, the choices made in the translations in question fail in my view to convey the conceptual scope (briefly expounded in the glossary provided below) of Lacoue-Labarthe's use of certain terms (for example, *citation*, *émoi*).

From a stylistic perspective, readers may note the use in this volume of contractions ("I'm," "don't," "isn't," "hasn't," "doesn't," "couldn't," and so on) and other markers of oral expression affecting syntax and rhythm (spacing, emphasis, quotation marks, punctuation, enumeration, recapitulation, parenthetical asides, etc.). In no way is the purpose of using, maintaining, or indeed exploiting such markers here to make the texts sound offhand or unconsidered. There is never a sense that these or any other texts by Lacoue-Labarthe engage in any complacency of this kind. On the contrary, the sober gravity and rigor of his thought, of his voice, preclude it outright. It is hoped, on the other hand, that, for better or for worse, retaining and resorting to oral markers such as those mentioned affords readers some inkling of the orality at play in Lacoue-Labarthe's thought, not just in terms of how that thought was delivered or intended to be delivered but also with regard to the philosophical implications of the spoken form. Obviously, this is not the place to comment on what is at stake here, which would deserve a volume of its own. It is worthwhile noting, however, if only to signpost areas that could be explored elsewhere, that it is no accident that the majority of the texts collected in this volume were not only written for oral delivery but preserved as such in their definitive form and that the majority of those that were not composed to this effect fundamentally entail the question of orality. This, in turn, implies a question of genre (the present volume alone spans a variety of generic categories: the book, the prologue, the academic conference paper, the personal address, the public reading paying homage, the journal article, the survey response, the interview, the poem), which raises further translation issues that call for more attention than can be spared in this note.

Another stylistic feature is worth noting here: what Alain Badiou referred to as Lacoue-Labarthe's "sharp, almost peremptory sentences," his "cutting, assertorial phrases."[2] The economy of Lacoue-Labarthe's dense style can sound unseemly when carried over into English. In spite of this, and at the risk of occasional awkwardness, here, too, I have tried to keep to Lacoue-Labarthe's distinctive voice, preferring at times unusually short, blunt sentences to the natural prolixity of the English language. That said, Lacoue-Labarthe's cutting style does not preclude agonizingly long-winded sentences, accumulating commas, colons, semicolons, dashes, em dashes, parentheses, precautions, qualifications, quotations, and so on, as if to make up for—or rather, *desist* from—the seeming peremptoriness of certain formulations. Here again, I have made every effort to echo the syntax of his voice—the parataxis of his thought.

★

Unless specified otherwise, author's footnotes are indicated in the asterisk-dagger sequence; endnotes of the translator and of the editors of the French text appear in Arabic numerals. As a general rule, glosses have been kept to a minimum and serve principally to refer to works (where traceable) quoted by the author. References to existing English translations, which have all been more or less modified for the present volume, are provided in the notes for works cited by the author and the editors of the French text, followed by references to the original. (Full bibliographical details on existing English translations are also given in the Bibliographical Note.) Where translations were available, titles cited by the author and the editors of the French text have been given in English. Occasional square brackets with brief comments appearing in the footnotes are the translator's.

Every translation agonizes over its impossibility. *Ending and Unending Agony* is no exception—not just because Lacoue-Labarthe, in his obstinate struggle for clarity, has a tendency to antagonize the structures and configurations of his own language but also because the English language does not always offer equivalents that neatly encompass the concepts carried by certain French terms or phrases frequently employed by Lacoue-Labarthe, often themselves already translated from the Greek, Latin, or German. As a result, original French terms or phrases have occasionally been given in square brackets immediately after the translated term or phrase in question. (Unless indicated otherwise, all other square brackets in the body of the text are the author's or, in the case of the Introduction, those of the editors of the French text.) But because this is not always sufficient, a brief glossary is provided below to help readers navigate some of the conceptual eddies peculiar to Lacoue-Labarthe's thinking.

Citer, citation, (le) citationnel

In Lacoue-Labarthe's lexicon, beyond denoting the ordinary practice of reproducing or transcribing a portion of text or speech in quotation marks, these terms can carry far-reaching philosophical implications, in which case, echoing a well-known essay by Thomas Mann on Freud,[3] they designate the repetition, in a given text, of "mythic schemata or sequences," or what Lacoue-Labarthe also refers to as "originary" or "matrix scenes." According to Lacoue-Labarthe, such "mythic citations" produce figures, models, or examples that, beyond being an aesthetic feature or indeed condition of works of art, have decisive political and ethical consequences insofar as they are capable of inducing human behavior. Where this philosophical (ethico-political) dimension tends to be implied, I have by and large reverted to literalness, thereby translating "to cite," "citation," and "(the) citational."

É-loignement, é-loigné

É-loignement is a rendering of Heidegger's *Ent-fernung*, the German prefix of which (*ent-*) oscillates between an intensification and a negation of the substantive (*Fernung*, that is, distancing, estrangement). Elsewhere, Lacoue-Labarthe describes *Ent-fernung* as involving a paradoxical logic—what he also calls a "hyperbologic"—whereby an augmentation (of the distancing or estrangement) is determined by an infinitely reverse relation (accentuating proximity).[4] Heidegger's term has been variously translated in English as "distance," "dis-distance," "de-distance," "dis-stance," "dis-stancing," and so on. André Préau's French translation, with which Lacoue-Labarthe was of course familiar,[5] steers clear of terms molded from "distance" and offers instead *recul* (that is, a step back or retreat). But a note in Préau's translation also suggests the more literal *dés-éloignement*,[6] which evidently provided the basis for Lacoue-Labarthe's own rendering. It seemed therefore preferable for the present translation to follow Lacoue-Labarthe's efforts to simplify and unclutter Préau's *dés-éloignement* and revert to "e-strangement" (or "e-stranged" for the adjective).

Émoi

While ordinarily suggesting turmoil, agitation, effervescence, excitement, or effusion, at any rate something of the order of affective energy, *émoi* takes on a more complex meaning in Lacoue-Labarthe's thought. It draws on its Old French etymon *esmai*—a substantive of *esmayer* (to trouble, disturb), which stems from the Vulgar Latin *exmagare* (to divest of power or ability), itself a combination of the Latin privative prefix *ex-* (out, out of) and the Old High German *magan* (to be powerful or able). In Lacoue-Labarthe's lexicon, then, the term, probably borrowed from Lacan's seminar *Anxiety*,[7] suggests almost the opposite of—or at least something entirely different from—what it might typically suggest. It connotes an experience that does not so much pertain to or is not so much carried by commotional energy or force but indicates instead a kind of lapsing, weakening, or flagging: an *impouvoir* (disempowerment),[8] as Lacoue-Labarthe also puts it.[9] In other words, what takes place as *émoi* in Lacoue-Labarthe does not *move* the subject undergoing it, lead to a *reaction*, and thus *empower* the subject; instead, eroding all forms of emotional empowerment, it opens the subject (or what is left of it) onto what Lacoue-Labarthe calls, in his eponymous "poem"—or rather "phrase" (see the corresponding entry below)—collected in this volume, "boundless indifference." Closely connected therefore with other key terms appearing in that phrase-poem—*détérioration* (deterioration), *dégradation* (degradation), *affaiblissement* (weakening), *défaillance* (failing), *déchéance* (decay), and so on—the word might be said to designate a mode of inspiration without pathos, divested of energy (in the strict sense of the term: activity, operation, work), thereby also bearing a relation to what Blanchot calls *désœuvrement* (commonly translated as "worklessness" or "unworking"). More specifically, *émoi* can be said to denote a mode of writing—a *phrase*, precisely—withdrawn, or in a process of withdrawing, from Western figuration and mythification mechanisms, in other words, as an interruption of art traditionally understood. Felicitously, the English language has a near equivalent in the term "dismay," which shares the same root as *émoi* and also combines a Latin privative prefix—*dis-* (out, without)—with the Old High German *magan*. Although "dismay" typically implies a loss of moral courage or resolution in the prospect of danger or difficulty, a meaning that is not essentially at stake here (but Lacoue-Labarthe's acceptation of *émoi* is also far from conventional in French), it does translate the absence or deprivation of strength or means etymologically at play in Lacoue-Labarthe's use of the term. However, it is impossible to render another related meaning Lacoue-Labarthe doubtless has in mind that resonates only with the French word (and may, for that matter, also bear a relation to what Artaud once termed an "in-affect *émoi*"):[10] *é-moi*, that is, without (the) self. Taking place within the self, it therefore also paradoxically describes an experience *outside* the subject: "within me outside me," to borrow Lacoue-Labarthe's expression in the phrase-poem, what he also refers to as "the caesura of the subject."[11]

(En) instance, instant

As Lacoue-Labarthe briefly points out in the present volume, the term *instance* may refer to at least four areas of signification: one is specifically time bound, as in the locution *en instance*, which indicates what is due, waiting, pending, or in abeyance, for example, "courrier en instance" (mail due to be dispatched), "un train en instance de départ" (a train about to leave), and so on. A second arises in the discourse of (Freudian) psychoanalysis to denote the agencies organizing the psychic apparatus, as in "les instances topiques du ça, moi et surmoi" (the topographical agencies of the id, ego, and superego). A third relates to the judiciary, as in the expressions "introduire en instance" (to institute legal proceedings), "être en instance" (when a matter is *sub judice*), or "les instances judiciaires" (the legal authorities), a meaning that appears also in English (a court of first instance, for example). A fourth pertains to (Benvenistian) linguistics, as in the notion of "les instances du discours," which designates acts by which language is actualized in speech by a speaker. As Bianchi and Kharlamov observe in the present volume, Lacoue-Labarthe's unpublished seminar series "L'instance de la mort" focuses on three other *instances*—the instances of language, literature, and memory—which, Lacoue-Labarthe argues, are at play in Blanchot's later work. In a very broad sense, then, *instance* could be said to indicate an underlying agency, authority, imposition, or condition of possibility (time, psyche, justice, language, literature, memory, death, and so on). With few exceptions and in spite of sounding awkward in some places, literalness—"instance," "instant"—seemed preferable here. Not least for etymological reasons: both terms derive from the stem *sta-* (the Indo-European root that in Latin yields *stare*, that is, "to stand") and are closely associated in Lacoue-Labarthe's thinking with the erecting or *instantiating* function at work in Western aesthetics, inasmuch as (re)presentation—in art, or indeed in (metaphysical) thought more generally—can be (and has been) conceived as the erection of figures and, by extension, myths, with all the ethico-political implications such figuration and mythification processes entail. This is particularly relevant in relation to the German philosophical tradition, insofar as what Lacoue-Labarthe deems to be among the most powerful reflections on art, those of Hegel and Heidegger, have produced or established concepts—*Gestalt* (figure), *Gestell* (installation), respectively—that are etymologically and philosophically governed by the same instantiating mechanism or what Lacoue-Labarthe also calls an "onto-steleo-logy."[12] Lacoue-Labarthe expends a great deal of effort deconstructing and interrupting precisely that mechanism—a task or event that he occasionally terms *défiguration* (disfiguration) or, drawing on Adorno,[13] *démythologisation* (demythologization) and that Derrida even more accurately describes as *désistance* (desistance).[14] Which is also why in specific cases where literalness seemed inadequate etymology has been preserved as far as possible: for example, when Lacoue-Labarthe writes of the very last words of Blanchot's *The Instant of My Death* as opening onto "le vide de l'instance éternelle," I have rendered this: "the void of being brought to an eternal stand," the term resonating etymologically with both Blanchot's and Lacoue-Labarthe's *instance* while also indicating what is brought to a stand or pause, pending, in abeyance, delayed.

Opération

This term has been variously translated here as "manoeuvre," "treatment," "application," or "move." In Lacoue-Labarthe's lexicon, *opération* tends to indicate a dialectical movement, process, or method, leading to a sublation of some kind or other (say, Hegelian or romantic)—in other words, a *mise en œuvre* or putting to work: bluntly put, an effectuation whereby thought is said to gain an absolute perspective and mastery over its "content" by integrating and maintaining what it negates. Where possible and appropriate, preference was given to "manoeuvre" (rendered in the British English spelling), since the latter preserves the etymon of work (*oeuvre*), which is central to

Lacoue-Labarthe's use of the term while also suggesting, in its ordinary sense, a "calculation" (a term also employed by Lacoue-Labarthe in the present volume), that is, a scheme, ploy, or strategy of thought or writing ultimately implying control over its so-called subject matter. In this sense, *opération* might be said to be fundamentally at odds with Blanchot's *désœuvrement* or, more broadly, with deconstruction.

Phrase

Apart from denoting the commonplace construction in connected speech or writing that consists in a collection of linguistic elements producing a meaningful unit typically containing a subject and predicate (that is, a sentence), this term can carry crucial philosophical implications in Lacoue-Labarthe's thinking, in which case it is inscribed in his "oral" determination of literature, where orality—or what Lacoue-Labarthe, in a different context (that of his reading of Benjamin's reading of Hölderlin), also refers to as "prosaism" (*prosaïsme*) or "phrasing" (*phrasé*)[15]—is construed as a kind of transcendental condition of an art or writing freed from the mythological, thereby (impossibly) uncitable and gesturing toward an arch-ethics. Where it is given this conceptual weight, the term has been literally translated as "phrase." There are instances, however, where the distinction between the ordinary linguistic unit ("sentence") and the orally or prosaically determined concept ("phrase")—if indeed one can speak here of a "concept"—cannot be neatly drawn or, rather, where both meanings are equally at stake. In "Dismay," for example, "sentence" was reluctantly chosen over "phrase" (the former seemed there more idiomatically agreeable and reflected more closely the linguistic terminology mobilized in the paragraph in which it appears), despite the fact that it breaks the chain of musicological terms and notions that organize the previous paragraph and the "poem" as a whole ("phrase" being of course also a musicological term). It is worthwhile noting that the term is also the title of the collection of "poems" in which "Dismay" was republished in 2000 (*Phrase*), as well as of the "poem" itself: "Phrase V (Dismay)."[16]

Protestation

Given the philosophical—specifically, theologico-political—reach of *protestation* in Lacoue-Labarthe's terminology, "protest," too readily denoting empirical, day-to-day politics, was felt to be an inadequate rendering here. A literal translation—"protestation"—seemed again the better option, insofar as it mobilizes the juridical sphere, as do the term and its lexical relatives ("contestation," "attestation," "detestation," "testament," and so on) in different ways throughout the present volume. Of course, the word also has strong religious—namely, Protestant—connotations (one mustn't forget that Lacoue-Labarthe hailed from a Calvinist background) but extends here to the political and philosophical field, inasmuch as politics can be interpreted as being (onto-)theological in essence, regardless of whether it is secular or atheistic. Hence Lacoue-Labarthe's reference in the present volume to the "religion of politics." From this perspective, *protestation* involves a form of "defiance," in other words, contesting—or desisting from—all forms of what Lacoue-Labarthe calls "fideistic subjection," be it religious, political, philosophical, ethical, aesthetic, or economic.

Reprendre, reprise, repentir

Ordinarily, the verb *reprendre* means "to revise," "to take up (again)," "to amend," "to correct," "to rework." Preference has generally been given here to the latter, it being made up of the term "work," which suggests a dialectical gesture Lacoue-Labarthe doubtless has in mind when discussing Blanchot's revision of his text "A Primal Scene." Although they may also, via fragmentation and a host of typographical devices (parentheses, quotation marks, italics, etc.), indicate a deconstructive process, *reprendre* and its substantive *reprise* tend nevertheless to designate an economy of work and all that such an economy implies. This also explains Lacoue-Labarthe's caution when using the verb "deconstruct" in scare quotes to describe some of Blanchot's later (fragmentary) writings, reflecting his suspicion that a kind of *opération* (see the corresponding entry above) is nonetheless at play. As for *repentir*, also employed in the context of Blanchot's practice of reworking his earlier version of "A Primal Scene," it means both "repentance" (or, more loosely, "regret," in the sense that Blanchot repented or regretted the earlier version of the text in question and so, growing uneasy about it, felt compelled to justify—that is, rework or, rather, "unwork"—it a posteriori) and the sign of an alteration in a literary or artistic work, the visible trace of a mistake or of an earlier composition (technically speaking, a *pentimento*).

★

This translation is only one of the many important editorial projects of which Helen Tartar was so crucially supportive over the course of her career. Sadly, her untimely death has prevented her from following the last stages of a project in which she had been interested "for years," as she put it to me when I first approached her with the idea of translating Lacoue-Labarthe's book on Blanchot (the French publisher had originally announced *Agonie terminée, agonie interminable* for early 2004, but for reasons detailed in the Introduction publication was postponed until 2011). The present translation is therefore a tribute to her memory. At Fordham University Press I would also like to thank Thomas Lay, Eric Newman, and Bud Bynack for their assistance at different stages of the project. I am grateful to Claire Nancy for authorizing the translation of both *Agonie terminée, agonie interminable* and the other material included in this volume but not appearing in the French edition. I also thank the Éditions Galilée for granting the foreign rights for this translation. I am grateful to Pascal Possoz for allowing the transcription, translation, and publication of the two-part interview included in the Appendix. I would like to reserve particular thanks for Leonid Kharlamov and Aristide Bianchi, who have been invaluable sources of expertise, judgment, and encouragement and who also generously transcribed the aforementioned interview. I also thank Michael Holland for reading portions of the present translation, John McKeane for helping me trace a number of bibliographical references, and James Hanrahan for pulling me out of grammatical brambles. Finally, I wish to acknowledge she who does not wish to be acknowledged.

ENDING AND UNENDING AGONY

Introduction

Aristide Bianchi and Leonid Kharlamov

On February 25, 2003, the day following the announcement of Maurice Blanchot's death, Philippe Lacoue-Labarthe spoke on a radio program over the telephone:

> If there ever was a "break [*coupure*]" in Blanchot's trajectory—I don't like the term, but if there was a transformation, perhaps from the publication of *Death Sentence* onward (I say "perhaps," as this is a hypothesis), then it is the moment Blanchot became posthumous. With the understanding, that is, that death is the condition of possibility of life, that he was thus already dead, that in a sense he had an experience without experience—an experience of death that would forever remain impossible and to which, on several occasions I think, he drew relatively near. In particular, I have in mind Blanchot's two great texts written during those last few years, which in my view are his two great autobiographical texts: "A Primal Scene" and *The Instant of My Death*. But I'd like to add the following: in the same way as he had made Orpheus the secret center of *The Space of Literature*, this experience without experience—this unexperienced experience of that death which is prior to existence and which entails that existence itself is posthumous and that, although Maurice Blanchot has just died, he was dead even before he was born—is what I think allowed him to construct what I shall call (and it seems to me we ought, surely, to talk about this) the *modern myth of the writer*. Perhaps in spite of himself, doubtless in spite of himself, Blanchot has become an absolutely mythical figure of the modern writer. And it seems to me that this erection of the figure of the writer complies not with what he's been reproached for—his ruminations over death, his indulgence in death, etc. (there's no indulgence in that whatsoever)—but with something like the idea that the writer is he who writes while knowing he is already dead. It is the enunciative position of the writer that presupposes his anterior death—and that, to my mind, is the great modern literary myth.[1]

The bulk of what constitutes the divide charting the present book is condensed in these six or seven sentences—and, to begin with, the exclusive role assigned to the two autobiographical texts by Blanchot to which the book's two sections correspond.

Let us consider first what is referred to in this radio broadcast as writing's posthumous condition. Insofar as this condition is not, precisely, incidental, the present book, published here in its unfinished form, was not destined to become twice posthumous: with respect to Maurice Blanchot (1907–2003) and with respect to Philippe Lacoue-Labarthe (1940–2007). The earliest text included in this book is contemporaneous with the publication of *The Instant of My Death* in late 1994; the most recent, with the death of Blanchot in early 2003. It would, however, be an oversimplification to see this death as a hindrance that would have prevented Lacoue-Labarthe from bringing his book to an end. Announced by the publisher in early 2004, it was, admittedly, an unfinished project but one he had never abandoned. In drawing the mythical figure of the writer from the posthumous condition of writing, Lacoue-Labarthe's brief declaration indicates instead an obstacle, or at least a fundamental difficulty—that of myth, to which Blanchot was all the more riveted as he sought obstinately to free himself from it.

Drawing on archival material, this introduction will strive to sketch out gradually a picture of the stumbling block that contributed to the incompletion of this book even before the death of Lacoue-Labarthe. The said archives (which contain preparatory notes as well as correspondence, seminars, and public declarations) offer material of varying but insufficient degrees of completeness to allow for or warrant a separate publication. Which is also why we have resolved to quote at length a variety of passages, thereby allowing the reader to peruse the most decisive ones.

The marked ambivalence that runs through the late declaration quoted above—that is, the recognition of the radically posthumous condition of writing, immediately followed by the worry that this condition may become a figure in the wake of the writer's withdrawal—dominated Lacoue-Labarthe's relationship with Blanchot early on. Having a direct bearing on both literature and the political, this relationship coincided for Lacoue-Labarthe with Blanchot's simultaneous entrance into literature and politics. As he explained in notes written for a "Post-scriptum," it was in these precise terms that he considered Blanchot's thought from the beginning, paying attention both to his critical discourse—he had begun reading what he called "the three B's" (Barthes, Bataille, Blanchot) as of 1956 (the year of the Soviet intervention in Hungary)—and to his political stances:

> Of my generation, only a few of us—rather few I think, but still . . .—followed very attentively what is now called, not without condescension or ill will (and, it must be said, not without foolishness [*niaiserie*]), Maurice Blanchot's "political itinerary."
>
> "Of my generation" roughly refers to the Second World War generation: let's say, 1938 to 1944. Or rather, more accurately: the "generation of 1940." "Attentively" in no way means "devoutly": contrary to what people here and there insist on accusing us of, devotion remained foreign to us. What prompted our attention can be situated: not May 1958 (General de Gaulle's coup) but the following academic year (and here I refer the reader to the publication dates of the three issues of the review *Le 14 Juillet*; Maurice Blanchot's name—his signature—appeared in two of these issues).[2]

Returning to this initial encounter, Lacoue-Labarthe writes in the present book: "Deafened, that is to say, still *infans*, I thus heard it [Blanchot's voice] for the first time, forty years ago. I was thinking, like everyone else, in terms of vocation. I entertained the hope of a community."[3] This community never materialized or at least was of another order than that which involves an actual encounter, a direct dialogue, be it in absentia. Blanchot did not break off his withdrawal, did not extend it so as to include the possibility of a response, the expectation of which, as we shall come to see, he failed to meet at least once in a decisive way. All the same, Blanchot's and Lacoue-Labarthe's writings crossed each other on numerous occasions, such that they ended up forming a dialogue bringing together other names: Jean-Luc Nancy, Roger Laporte, Jacques Derrida, to name but those three. This long dialogue began dramatically in January 1976 when Blanchot gave his support to the review *Première Livraison* (set up by Lacoue-Labarthe and Mathieu Bénézet) by sending in his text—"A Primal Scene"—less than two weeks after the review was founded. The latter text, together with *The Instant of My Death*, would become the focus of the present book. But before addressing the book itself, it is worthwhile briefly indicating a few preliminary points of reference.

First of all, the dialogue had in a sense begun earlier via Roger Laporte, who had corresponded with Blanchot since the 1950s and who in 1972 had engaged in an intense exchange with Lacoue-Labarthe on the experience of writing, thereby swiftly establishing a lasting friendship. What Laporte calls "Biography"[4]—the notion of a life that is neither prior nor exterior to writing—would resonate constantly with what Lacoue-Labarthe's thought, in its attempt to engage with the resistance to autobiography found in Blanchot—that is, a writer who kept anecdotal narratives pertaining to the individual so obstinately at bay—sought to construe as the experience, in writing, of the disappearance or failing [*défaillance*]—of the death—of its subject.

Alongside the constant presence of Roger Laporte and the initial set of circumstances introduced by "A Primal Scene," one can make out at least three main threads governing Lacoue-Labarthe's dialogue with Blanchot. The first, from *The Literary Absolute*, written together with Jean-Luc Nancy, to *Misère de la littérature* to *The Writing of the Disaster*, unfolds the question of the birth, possibility, and end of literature.[5] The second thread, weaving its way through *The Nazi Myth* and "Intellectuals Under Scrutiny,"[6] opens up the question of the possibility of an exit [*sortie*] from myth. Finally, the third thread tackles head-on the question of the political. We shall address the latter thread first (the other two will emerge as we go along), which begins in 1984 when Lacoue-Labarthe and Nancy were given the opportunity to edit an issue of the *Cahiers de l'Herne* devoted to Blanchot. Lacoue-Labarthe presented the project to Blanchot in the following terms:

> One of our ideas—though in truth, it speaks for itself—would be to devote a section of the issue to the political question. But it would be something entirely different from the "dossier" sketched out (more or less successfully) a few years ago by the review *Gramma*,[7] something we view more readily as an opportunity for us (for our generation) to ask, through you, the question of the political in this century—and of the political responsibility of writing. Your example has long convinced us of the need to subject this question, more generally, to a radical reconsideration. To that effect, a few weeks ago I hesitated to propose to *Libération* a few pages regarding the publication in French of Jeffrey Mehlman's book[8] (the reasoning of which, as far as you are concerned, as far as your own trajectory is concerned, seems wrong to me, if only because at no point does the book take into account a difference of which Mehlman is the first to be aware: the difference between what pertains to discourse and what belongs to writing, in the sense that Derrida, for example, distinguishes these terms; not to mention, of course, the utter blindness to what a political experience, a political awareness [*conscience*], and a political conversion might entail—that is to say, also, to what a conversion *tout court* might entail; and I say nothing of his apparent ignorance of what, in Europe and since romanticism, radical nationalism represented—but his argument is itself romantic). But I think an article would not have been sufficient to contend with this task, and so I preferred to defer: to save it perhaps, should its necessity still be felt later, for the said issue of the *Cahiers de l'Herne*.[9]

The very same word of "conversion" would be employed by Lacoue-Labarthe when he specified to Dionys Mascolo exactly what, within the context of the political question, he proposed to examine in Blanchot. It is no easy task to extrapolate what this term, drawn from religious terminology, aims to suggest, but one can assume that Lacoue-Labarthe intends to explore, through Blanchot, the possibility of a radical experience of the political.[10] It is precisely this radicality that Lacoue-Labarthe foregrounds in the radio broadcast referred to in the opening of this introduction:

> To me, Blanchot has always represented the epitome of the aristocratic intellectual: extremely intransigent, extremely eloquent, and whose principal enemy will have always been what we call—without quite knowing any longer what we mean by this term—the bourgeoisie. And in a sense . . . well, I accept that in 1938 he stopped writing openly political texts, that in 1941, especially after his decisive encounter with Bataille [. . .], he sided with the Résistance, that he later opposed de Gaulle, that he wrote the "The Manifesto of the 121," that in 1968 he published a number of articles which no one knew were his. Well, today, we know all of this. . . . Very well then. But in my view there will have always been in Blanchot the same attitude of an extremely violent intransigence. I repeat this word that in no way precludes, I imagine (I have never met him, I think I have had only a couple telephone conversations with him regarding something relatively trivial, we exchanged a few words or rather letters), an extreme tenderness, an extreme kindness, which is to say an intelligence. But he is also . . . radical. To put it briefly. It is very difficult to speak about this. I have read a considerable number of his prewar texts: there's a side to them that is often strictly unbearable [*intolérable*] for people like "us." At the same time, the hostility toward Hitlerism, for instance, toward the specifically German form of fascism, is such that it is quite clear that in the end Blanchot is relatively unclassifiable within the French far right.[11]

Comparing the two extracts quoted above, it is worthwhile noting the ambivalence of the said radicality as it shifts between a certain continuity of an "exemplary trajectory" and the experience of a break. Perhaps the very meaning of this ambivalence encapsulates the question that Lacoue-Labarthe and Nancy sought to address to Blanchot. In the end, the question was never formulated. Following their suggestion of a dialogue—through an exchange of letters, should Blanchot have preferred to maintain his withdrawal—Blanchot replied on August 10, after having taken the time to think about it, that he did not exclude the possibility of such a dialogue. The dialogue never took place. Instead, as a preliminary, Blanchot addressed to them, via Laporte, a letter that the latter referred to as a "Memorandum," doubtless because it was more akin, despite its initial form of address, to a recapitulation. In it, Blanchot described, more than he questioned, his activities and positions before the war and during the Occupation. Published only recently,[12] Blanchot's indirect response did not meet their expectations. And for lack of contributors, the aforementioned project of the *Cahiers de l'Herne* would finally be abandoned the following summer.

It was undoubtedly a missed opportunity, one that in fact returned when, in 1992, Lacoue-Labarthe and Nancy planned to take up again the work begun around Blanchot and the question of the political and when Laporte passed on to them—with Blanchot's consent—other letters, drawn this time from his own correspondence. The latter material, together with the "Memorandum," thus added further to a kind of political testament. This project was abandoned as well, thereby leaving the demand that had prompted it intact, a demand the scope of which can no doubt be measured in light of the work Lacoue-Labarthe had carried out in the meantime around Heidegger in *The Fiction of the Political*.[13]

One can well appreciate, then, that the publication of *The Instant of My Death*, beyond the admiration it aroused from a literary standpoint, must have come as a shock, seeing as the book had taken up the place indicated, not without difficulty, by the said letters. In it, Blanchot told the story of the aforementioned conversion; it was now a question of interpreting this conversion, which is what Lacoue-Labarthe undertook to do (just as Jacques Derrida had done),[14] thereby initiating the present book. As a result, *The Instant of My Death* abruptly unlocked the political question, even while tying it, in the space of a brief narrative, to the other main threads mentioned earlier: the condition of literature and the demand of an exit from myth.

Let us therefore return to the aforesaid starting point of the dialogue with Blanchot. In 1976, in response to Lacoue-Labarthe's invitation to compose a text for *Première Livraison*, Blanchot sends him "A Primal Scene." Lacoue-Labarthe is struck with amazement. "This text has left me dumbfounded, speechless," he writes to Laporte on February 1. As a result, Lacoue-Labarthe would in a sense never cease responding to it: almost immediately, at first, and again much later. "Much later," that is: with the present book. "Almost immediately," that is: as early as summer 1976, with "Dismay,"[15] the genesis of which he describes to Laporte on August 23:

> I have resolved to send you without further delay the last two issues of *Première Livraison*, as well as a text I wrote for a small volume commissioned by Emmanuel Hocquard. Regarding the latter, it had to be short (it is already too long . . .): I have gone from approximately fifty pages to this—which in part explains the delay. Like the previous one,[16] I am passing it on to you so that you tell me, plainly, what you think of it. In fact, it is related to the previous

> one but retranscribed in prose, transformed, etc. It thus belongs to that *Oratio soluta* which may well never see the light of day. The bulk of it was written last October. Once I had finished it, I nevertheless realized that it somehow amounted to a kind of "response" to the text by Blanchot published in *Première Livraison*. How odd.

Consequently, "Dismay" is distinctly addressed—as a (initial) response to "A Primal Scene"—to Blanchot, who in September had consented to it being dedicated to him.

Having decided to include this text in the present volume, in the margins of the book proper (it is nowhere included in the book plans sketched out by Lacoue-Labarthe for *Ending and Unending Agony*), we shall not give a full commentary on it here. Several motifs put forward by Blanchot are at issue. First, the scene itself: can that which is said therein—an exit from the self without exit, an empty ecstasy—make up a scene? Second, the secret with which Blanchot's text almost comes to a close: "He says nothing. Henceforth he will live in the secret." Lacoue-Labarthe's response tilts the question toward the issue of the avowal but remains firm: "there is no secret." Finally, "Dismay" is the *phrase* that perhaps responds to the tears and to their drying up [*tarissement*]. We shall return to this later, for at stake here is a discussion that cannot be brought to a close and that would haunt Lacoue-Labarthe until the latter years of his life as he reached the edge of the project's incompletion. Hence our decision to reprint "Dismay" (published thirty years earlier) at the end of Lacoue-Labarthe's book.

The exchange does not end with "Dismay," since Blanchot in turn takes up these motifs in *The Writing of the Disaster*. The interlocutors of the dialogic passages where, fragment after fragment, Blanchot progressively probes, reworks, and reframes the terms of "A Primal Scene" are numerous, and their names are not given; however, one recognizes, among others, Lacoue-Labarthe.[17] Strangely, this reworking by Blanchot did not give rise to a response from Lacoue-Labarthe. Once again, a response would not be given until after the publication of *The Instant of My Death* some fifteen years later.

Everything in "A Primal Scene" entitled and beckoned Lacoue-Labarthe to write "on" Blanchot. But something in this text and in its reworked version placed at the heart of *The Writing of the Disaster* held him back, something for which *The Instant of My Death* provided a release (as well as a constraint), something, evidently, that gave cause for disquiet or discussion and that, occasionally, he happened to formulate:

> "A Primal Scene": to say that I have read and reread these few lines is an understatement. I know them by heart; they have haunted me, dwelt in me, as

a musical phrase alone is capable of doing. And if I thought I could discern in it a kind of "solicitation [*appel*]," it is precisely because I heard in it something I recognized—as if through an echo, assuming I cannot avoid giving in, once again, to one of my oldest demons. Always the same one, in truth. However, there was also, in these few lines, something that remained indecipherable. And if it took me almost twenty years to venture a commentary on it—feeling suddenly compelled to do so as a result of the publication of and receiving *The Instant of My Death*—it is not so much because the opportunity didn't present itself or because the publication, in the meantime, of a second version seemed to me to complicate the task seriously and make it too difficult (it is precisely this second version that will draw my attention here). Rather, it is because a muted resistance—discernible in "Dismay," besides—held me back, hindered, or prevented me; a resistance that was the less difficult to acknowledge as it was also a resistance to my own propensity.

Let me briefly explain.

In the address itself, the *withdrawal* [retrait] (in both senses of the term) of the "I" or of the so-called subject of enunciation; in the passage to the third-person singular (the child), the recalling of the birth—if not the "primal scene"—of literature (the Freudian reference didn't seem to me awkward at all), in accordance with the analysis of it proposed by Blanchot in well-known passages from *The Space of Literature*; the motif of the pane, and of the broken pane, which suddenly brought back the memory of Blanchot's narratives; the ecstasy, that is, the revelation without revelation, which was bound to recall the paradoxical experience of no-thingness [*né-ant*], according to Heidegger, in other words, *Erfahrung* par excellence, were it not for the extremely precise "atheological" allusion to or quasi quotation of Bataille; the secret, now broken, but in order to explain the strange, erstwhile decision through which, in his refusal to yield to tears or in their drying up, access to what Blanchot for a long time now no longer called "literature" but *writing* was granted: all of this, yes, even the triviality or banality of the occasion, I understood, I recognized—within my capabilities, that is, and precisely because I wasn't *myself* implicated, I could regard it as "mine." It involved an emotion that is absolutely anterior.

This emotion—and not dismay [*émoi*], I admit—stemmed also from the fact that up until then, to my knowledge at least, this text was the only text by Blanchot that could be described as autobiographical, almost in the mode of a confession (I'm thinking of Augustine, Rousseau, to whom I had always been very close), and that I couldn't stop being surprised at the fact that our invitation, so e-stranged [*é-loignée*], would become the occasion for the publication of this "autobiographical prose poem," as I called it then.

Nevertheless, this emotion, in truth, came from elsewhere. From another

> "event." It came from the joy and the tears (the "ravaging joy," the "endless stream of tears"); but it was also here, and I knew this immediately, that the said resistance began to form. It was not so much that such lines accentuated, or even made explicit, perhaps too much so, the text's adherence to a tradition reputed to be "mystical." After all, if I was *touched*, it was for this very reason. And at any rate, the lines in question were strictly delimited: on the one hand, by the reference to the empty ecstasy, in truth overtranslated from Heidegger (*Nichts ist was es gibt*), and on the other, including perhaps some reservations about Levinas's understanding of the "there is" ["*il y a*"], by the final drying up [*assèchement*], a refusal or (who knows) an acknowledgment of powerlessness, which announces—but doesn't promise—the "desert": of writing. Or so I gathered. No, what caused my resistance was, in more muted fashion, the reference to a *certain* mystical tradition, a form of devotion—essentially French, it seems to me—based entirely on effusion (the trace of which can be followed at least up to Rousseau) and consequently sentimental. A tradition of which Pascal's *Memorial* ("Joy! Joy! Tears of joy . . ."), which had, precisely, been kept secret and been discovered, as is known, in the lining of his coat following his death, offers the most spectacular example (and it so happens, in my childhood, the most compelling).
>
> Those tears, the crying, was a citation of Pascal. I couldn't come to terms with it . . . I was stuck, I admit, perplexed.[18]

Drawn from a conference paper that remains unspecified, this long quotation indicates that it was Blanchot's adherence to a mystical tradition based on effusion that stood in the way. Through this adherence, Blanchot ended up repeating the program of a certain kind of literature. However, concurrent with this disquiet, one cannot fail to mention another of Lacoue-Labarthe's reservations, this time about the fragmentary mechanism of *The Writing of the Disaster*, which, in its own way, also repeated a literary program—that of romanticism. This reservation is inscribed in what we identified earlier as the first thread of the dialogue that unfolds from *The Literary Absolute* onward.

If *The Literary Absolute* traced the origin of the modern project of literature to the romantic project of the novel and the fragment, it also, conversely, marked a radical closure of the possibility of these two forms. As with all closures, this did not imply that it was no longer possible to write in fragments; rather, it implied that one could not assign renouncement to the absolute, or worklessness [*désœuvrement*], to the negativity of the fragmentary form. Lacoue-Labarthe and Nancy made a point of this when reacting explicitly to the publication of *The Writing of the Disaster* in a text entitled "*Noli me frangere*" (that is, do not break me apart, do not fragment me).[19] In this text, written deliberately—at the limit of the possibilities it indicates—in the romantic form of a series of fragmented dialogues, one reads, in response to a quotation drawn from Blanchot,[20] the following rejoinder:

> I'm grateful that you give Blanchot credit for having avoided (or *known how* to avoid?) the "twofold trap" of "overdialectization" and "overfragmentation." But a dialectic—even supplementary, even negative—remains a dialectic. That is to say, an economy. Basically, I'm having difficulty understanding the sentence by Blanchot on which you're basing your remarks; for, if I follow you, the said sentence seems to you best to translate "the fragmentary demand" (as opposed to the "fragmentary will" of the romantics); I'm having difficulty understanding the phrase "it maintains itself as the energy of disappearing"—that sort of negative sublation [*relève*] which would make no sense if it weren't precisely an *energy* that was *maintained*: a putting to work [*mise en œuvre*]. There is still will there (besides, is it avoidable?) and therefore also, probably, a calculation, the ruse of a final calculation: that of the incalculable.[21]

If the reworking of "A Primal Scene" in *The Writing of the Disaster* destabilizes primitiveness [*primitivité*], the secret, or the scene, at what cost, and thanks to which power, to which putting to work, does this take place? "*Noli me frangere*" practically ends with the following dialogue:

> —I meant to say that the fragment, even in Blanchot, is too much the mark of the Modern. It is impossible to tear it free from the Modern . . .
>
> —From Nietzsche, for example, who plays a large role in the origins of Blanchot's "fragmentary writing." In short, if you mean there is nothing to be done with the fragment as such (that is, ultimately, with the fragment as *genre*) . . .
>
> —Yes, but not with fragmentation . . .
>
> —I quite understand. No, the fragment as genre is still the will to fragment, with everything that entails: *literature*, in its very delimitation: the letter of the subject. With Barthes, it is striking: Montaigne, the recurrence of self-portraiture. And as for Blanchot's anonymous self-effacement . . .
>
> —That's something else again. How could one reduce anonymity to self-portraiture, were it even that of the subject of literature?[22]

The fragment as such continues to carry with it literature and the subject that come to inscribe their effacement in the fragment. More obscurely still: returning, via this detour, to Pascal's tears, to what extent does the fragment carry the effusion of the subject insofar as it distributes (or draws out?) that effusion? Here again, the publication of *The Instant of My Death* comes to interrupt the "plastic" force of the fragment by giving way, via a narrative—one last time—to the lightness [*légèreté*] of an "exit from the self." It thus inextricably opens up the possibility of "its" commentary and that of "A Primal Scene." In turn, this renouncement of the fragment, concurrent with the vertiginous departure from the kind of factual synopsis exhibited by the "Memorandum," makes *The Instant of My Death* the testamentary text that Lacoue-Labarthe (and Jacques Derrida) had taken it to be: a last will and testament as political as it was literary.

★

The present unfinished book was thus born of the necessity of linking a reading of "A Primal Scene" to that of *The Instant of My Death*—or, rather, as we have seen and as the book itself presents it, of *The Instant of My Death* to that of "A Primal Scene." Through a determined and necessary gesture that brings these two texts together, Lacoue-Labarthe makes it possible for their titles to translate each other and for the "instant" to respond more directly to the said "scene" than one might at first imagine. If *Ending and Unending Agony* is an unfinished book, it is not because it lacks a definitive form: its structure is clear, in light of both its project and Lacoue-Labarthe's book plans, which we have followed scrupulously. This is readily apparent in the fact that the brief "blurb," converted here into a "Prologue" and written originally to present the project, corresponds exactly to the book.

According to the book plans and the notes left behind, two texts are missing; these would have featured in the first section of the book (focused on *The Instant of My Death*) as the section's third chapter—under the title "Cryptie"—and third annex—"Manet."

Lacoue-Labarthe left no notes for "Manet." There is, however, little doubt that the starting point for the piece would have been Manet's *Execution of Maximilian*, which reworks Goya's *Third of May* and which in 1955 was the subject of a long commentary in Bataille's *Manet* entitled "The Destruction of the Subject." The parallel between Blanchot's narrative and Manet's painting does not simply have to do with the similarity of what might be said therein (the suspended gunfire during an execution) but relates to the fact that, in their presentation of the most extreme and meaningful moment—the putting to death of the subject—an absolute detachment from any form or will of speaking [*volonté du dire*] is revealed: "In principle, death, when dealt out methodically, cold-bloodedly, by soldiers, does not go hand in hand with indifference: it is a subject charged with meaning, producing a violent feeling. But Manet appears to have depicted the subject as insensitive; the spectator accompanies him in a profound apathy. This painting recalls the numbing of a tooth: from it emanates an impression of engulfing numbness."[23] Blanchot's "lightness" responds to Bataille's "indifference"—indifference being Manet's very *secret*, as he puts it, that which produces the silence of his paintings; it is as if, in both cases, existence were silently laid bare by the stay of execution.

As for the crypteia—literally, as Amyot remarked, "the secret one, as you might say"—it denotes a Lacedaemonian institution, known by Plato and Plutarch, that has been the subject of constant debate among scholars of classical antiquity, some hesitating to attribute a military function to it, others seeing it as nothing other than the regulated game of a violent initiation rite.[24] Its distinctive traits are the following: wandering, expulsion from the city and from its comforts and rules, the prohibition of being seen, and the arbitrary nocturnal murders of enemies reduced to servitude known as the Helots. Young men from Sparta were thus sent off to live in the mountains and in the woods at the edge of the city, where, in a kind of rite of passage, they take to the maquis, as it were, which is not without recalling the journey described in Blanchot's narrative.

In choosing this title—"Crypteia"—borrowed from the terminology of initiation, Lacoue-Labarthe blots out the terms "crypt" (which would tend to localize) and "encryption" (which would tend to highlight an intention). According to the notes left in his papers, Lacoue-Labarthe was directly targeting the strange confusion in dates—which had in fact been immediately noticed and discussed, in particular by Derrida[25]—disrupting the "historical" import of *The Instant of My Death* to the extent that one can say that fragmentation creeps into the dating scheme via the very movement that enables the primal scene to attain the clarity of the narrative.

In a note from 2003, dated "Monday 13 October, 197th anniversary—to the day—of the Battle of Jena," Lacoue-Labarthe writes the following:

> Disbelief, at first, if not astonishment. And then, quickly, almost immediately—it is inevitable—suspicion; or at least the question: what happened? What did he have in mind, or what had he allowed to happen? These few lines, I know full well, have often been singled out and commented on since their publication seven years[26] ago. I quote them once again, however, as they have withstood all elucidation:
>
> "When the lieutenant returned and became aware that the young lord of the manor [*châtelain*] had disappeared, why did anger, rage, not prompt him to burn down the Château (immobile and majestic)? Because it was the Château. On the façade was inscribed, like an indestructible reminder, the date 1807. Was he cultivated enough to know this was the famous year of Jena, when Napoleon,

on his small grey horse, passed under the windows of Hegel, who recognized in him the 'spirit of the world,' as he wrote to a friend?"

And in another note:

The error made about the date of the Battle of Jena and the year of publication of the *Phenomenology of Spirit* leaves no doubt, right from the start: this "error" is not an error, or if it is, it is calculated; it involves a strange commemorative cryptography: 1807–1907: the birth of Maurice Blanchot. Likewise, the date of the colophon of the first edition of *The Instant of My Death* (22 September 1994) makes it impossible for even a remotely attentive reader to remain indifferent: on that day, Maurice Blanchot turned 87.

In his "biographical essay," Christophe Bident reveals some useful facts on this cryptographic (haunting) obsession,[27] namely in relation to *Death Sentence* (published in 1948, but recounting "events" that took place in 1938 (?)). But see also "Kafka and the Work's Demand":

"If, up until 1912, he does not devote himself entirely to literature, he gives himself this excuse: 'I cannot take the risk as long as I have not succeeded in completing a more substantial work, capable of satisfying me fully.' The night of 22 September 1912 brings him this success, this proof. That night he writes *The Verdict* in one stretch. It brings him unmistakably near the point where it seems that 'everything can be expressed, that for everything, for the strangest of ideas a great fire is ready in which they perish and disappear.'"[28]

The said "mania" is therefore longstanding. But I shall stick to *The Instant of My Death* alone. Here too, Christophe Bident has conducted a discerning investigation: the "residence [*demeure*]" mentioned (the "Château"), in Quain, does not bear the date 1807 on its façade, but 1809; and as for the date of the episode in question or rather of the incident [*péripétie*], it was probably not, as Maurice Blanchot had nevertheless claimed in a letter to Jacques Derrida, that of 20 July ("20 July. Fifty years ago, I knew the happiness of nearly being shot dead")[29] but that of 20 June.

If one sets aside the hypothesis of some kind of haunting obsession with coincidence, keeping count, commemoration, or even superstitious dating; if one can legitimately consider as minor the hypothesis of a lapse of memory accentuated by age (was it already at stake in 1948 or in 1958?)[30] or of a propensity for "misrepresentation [*travestissement*]" (since the word, I think, has been used), the concept of "mythomania," on the other hand, provided one rids it of its psychological dross, seems most fitting.

One can however surmise that at play here is not "false testimony" (that would be absurd) but a specific chronological "fictionalization [*fictionnement*],"

> as the kind occasionally resorted to in myth—and in any case in most of the great examples of automythicization, of testimony "without attestation" (and to begin with, that of Malraux). Such is what *must* be named *poetry*.

The sketch breaks off here, with the following indication: "'mythic transposition' *The Infinite Conversation*, p. 166," which refers to the second text Blanchot devotes to Simone Weil in the book section entitled "The Limit-Experience." The text discusses an "event" (that of her mystical experience), the narrative—or "Prologue"—of which is, according to Blanchot's expression, a "mythic transposition." Describing Weil's concern to prevent this event from turning into a show of authority, Blanchot writes:

> Besides, when one would wish for it to act as proof, it is no longer the experience that is present but its memory. And the memory of a mystical event is not mystical; rather, it reintroduces, among the uncertainties of time and discourse, the ungraspable certainty of which memory is but a reflection. Or to put it more precisely, a memory is valid only through the transformation of those who remember and to the extent to which they would be able to become entirely that of which there is memory. But then they would no longer remember. They would become oblivion, a void, a pure nothing, for them and for us.[31]

We reach here the crux of Lacoue-Labarthe's unease: does the confusion in dates correspond to a process of fictionalization, of automythicization, of the said mythic transposition? The entire book, in both its culmination and incompletion, is caught between the two movements—in Blanchot—of mythicization and demythologization. Within this tension, the figure of Malraux, unexpectedly introduced at the very end of *The Instant of My Death*, acts alternately as paradigm and foil. For, clearly, Blanchot did not place his narrative under the sign of Napoleon's passing through Jena so as to place himself under the aegis of History's Grand Narrative, to which Hegel consents when he recognizes in him the spirit of the world passing through on his horse; at worst, he is placing himself under the aegis of its impossibility.

The unease and difficulty here come from the fact that it would be futile to criticize hastily the "mythic transposition," the fictionalization of dates, and the transformation of memory in the testamentary text of a writer who, with obstinate determination, never ceased combating myth. At the end of "Fidelities," the first text of this book, Lacoue-Labarthe links this difficulty to the need to question the "now famous proposition" in "Intellectuals Under Scrutiny" according to which "in the Jew, in the 'myth of the Jew,' what Hitler wanted to annihilate was, precisely, mankind freed from myths."[32] The question Derrida addressed to Lacoue-Labarthe after he gave his paper points precisely to this unease, which makes it impossible to decide between mythicization and demythicization:

> This moment of "resurrection" in Montaigne, in Rousseau, in Blanchot, [. . .] this moment he described because of its lightness (so well expressed by all three of them) is like a moment of deliverance or innocence. And you said: "deliverance, not in the religious sense of redemption"—although in "deliverance," there is precisely absolution, *Erlösung*, which means salvation [. . .]. So, in that moment of *Erlösung*, of deliverance—and this is where I'm having difficulty understanding the direction of the steps you were taking at that moment—is that a mythical moment or a moment in which myth dissolves?[33]

And the question was immediately coupled with a doubt cast over the phrase "mankind freed from myth," which Blanchot glimpses, negatively, through the object of Nazi persecution:

> Judaism is not one, single thing; there are Judaisms, there are currents, there are interpretations, there are heresies, etc.—but never would I be prepared to subscribe to such a sweeping statement as "Judaism breaks with myth" or "is innocent of a logic of sacrifice."

To which Lacoue-Labarthe replied:

> I think Blanchot is trying here to free *himself* from the mythical via a gesture that is both simple and complicated, which consists in naming Malraux, who played an important part as far as myth is concerned (in fact an enormous part, and in a rather emphatic style—far worse than what I'm capable of). He tries this by availing of the following proposition on Nazi anti-Semitism advanced in "Intellectuals Under Scrutiny," a text which I think dates back to 1984: "Hitler went after the people who freed themselves from myth."
>
> And the logic of what I meant to say was this: I must question that and I won't accept it—in the same way as when you asked me (after I had said that the Shoah wasn't sacrificial): "Are you so sure of that?", I thought about it and said to myself: "He was right." I, too, cannot accept the proposition: "the Jews . . .", or, as he even says, "the Jew . . ." I cannot say that, I have heard it too often. Blanchot begins by saying "Judaism," then "the Jewish people," and then "the Jew, who is being punished for having freed himself from myth." I don't believe it. It is no doubt very complicated, and I don't have the means to ascertain it nor to do the enormous work required in order to distinguish from one another, as you say, Judaisms, interpretations of Judaism, different traditions . . . I believe there is myth, the fact of myth, and that one cannot for a moment imagine a religion—in the most general sense of the term, or the most

universal, as Bataille used to say in his ethnological spontaneity—without myth. And that no one can escape it.

I don't want to call into question the sort of probity at stake in this very complicated kind of manoeuvre [*opération*] attempted here by Blanchot—I borrow Nietzsche's term because I can't find a more suitable one and despite the fact that I well appreciate Blanchot's strategic—if not cunning—side. But I didn't want to make the simple move that would consist in saying: "Blanchot represents the return to myth and he never left that sphere," or "Blanchot represents pure innocence vis-à-vis myth and that's what he sought to affirm." I meant to say instead: on the question of myth—and that's indeed what drew my attention to everything that takes place around "A Primal Scene," given that the latter is the only other autobiographical narrative he has written in the past few years, that is, openly or almost openly autobiographical—something is happening in Blanchot. Around this question of fiction, of myth, of the primal scene, he clearly encounters a difficulty: he goes through Leclaire again, he summons Ovid, he speaks of narcissism, he even ventures into the psychoanalytic field whereas usually he practically never speaks of it, he calls on Winnicott as well, etc. I think it is because this poses a problem for him.

My own gesture did not amount to excuse Blanchot—if such a proposition has any meaning, and if indeed it falls to any of us to do such a thing—nor did it amount to accuse him once again of having had a hand in this whole affair regarding myth—for we all have a hand in it. I simply meant to say that it seems to me that Blanchot is one of the few to have perceived that therein lies a difficulty—I shall put it thus, in very simple terms: he perceived this—and that the last texts he wrote, his last reflections on the mythical, on fiction, allow us to grasp this perception. I didn't want it to be too long, but I wanted to add another paragraph on that quotation from "Intellectuals Under Scrutiny" regarding Jews as a people without myth. I wanted to say: perhaps without idols, I can well believe it, but not without myth, certainly not. And not without sacrifice either, certainly not.

Five years earlier, in July 1992—and here we come to the second thread of the dialogue we mentioned earlier (that of the exit from myth)—having returned to the question regarding Blanchot and the political, Lacoue-Labarthe and Nancy had included an annex to *The Nazi Myth*, introducing the following point:

> We shall limit ourselves to observing here that at stake is no doubt less a wish to affirm that "the Jew is without myth"—an affirmation that would in any event require detailed examination—as a need to be attentive to a secret reversal that could, in turn, make of the proposition "without myth"—and therefore also of the proposition "the Jew"—a new myth.[34]

This marks the beginning of a response to Blanchot as much as it indicates a return to this or the other passage from the book itself:

> In this regard [in regard to the fact that if the Nazi myth was initially determined as the myth of the "race," it is because it is also the myth of Myth, that is, the myth of the creative power of myth in general], it is essential to note that the Jew [in Nazi ideology] is not simply a bad race, a defective type: he is the antitype, the bastard par excellence. He has no culture of his own, Hitler says, nor even a religion of his own, for monotheism predates him. The Jew has no *Seelengestalt* (no form or figure to constitute a soul) and thus no *Rassengestalt* (no form or figure to constitute a race): his form is formless. The Jew is the man of the universal abstract, as opposed to the man of singular, concrete identity. Which is why Rosenberg takes care to point out that the Jew is not the "antipode" of the German but his "contradiction," by which he no doubt means that the Jew is not an opposite *type* but the very absence of type, a danger present in all bastardizations, which all are parasitic.[35]

To say, by inference, that Blanchot would have somehow adopted Rosenberg's Jew by inverting the value of the proposition "without myth" or "without type" is overhasty. Furthermore, the 1992 annex referred the reader to another conference paper given by Lacoue-Labarthe and Nancy, entitled "The Jewish People Do Not Dream," which closely followed the first version of *The Nazi Myth*.[36] We quote from the second section of the paper, delivered by Lacoue-Labarthe:

> The Jewish people do not constitute a subject—and there is no being-Jewish-proper [*être-proprement-juif*]. But this is not to be understood in the sense in which Nietzsche, in the wake of Plato's (or Diderot's) mimetology, could argue that the Jew—like the actor or the woman—is the mimetic being par excellence who, being nothing by himself, is "fit for all roles and characters" (the expression here is Diderot's). For that is precisely what Freud combats in Nazi anti-Semitism: the imputation of impropriety as the proper. Instead, what must be understood is that the Jews, because of the aforesaid lack of a subject, are bearers of the revelation that no social formation or political institution, whatever it may be (a people or a nation, to remain with the field discussed by Freud), is ever capable of accomplishing itself as a subject. There is, in general terms, no realized political identity.[37]

It is worthwhile noting that the proposition "this is not to be understood in the sense in which . . ." is as much an injunction aimed at himself as it is hermeneutic cautioning. If the heart of the matter is the impossibility of realizing social formation into a subject or the impossibility of a political (or theological) identity, one can appreciate why, a few weeks following the discussion with Derrida at Cerisy, Lacoue-Labarthe could return obliquely, and in a different context (he was responding to a survey on intellectuals conducted by the review *Lignes* entitled "Les intellectuels, tentative de définition par eux-mêmes"),[38] to the discussion around the problematic proposition in "Intellectuals Under Scrutiny." His response takes once again a "detour" via Malraux, thereby recontextualizing the definition of the intellectual given by Blanchot even while indicating his refusal to turn Auschwitz into an absolute:

> I shall limit myself simply to the following, which, besides, Blanchot does not fail to suspect—albeit laterally—as well: if anti-Semitism has been (and remains) de facto the fault line of this catastrophic century [. . .], it did not take the modern formulation of the "Jewish question" for intellectual *protestation* to manifest itself. It is essentially for having defended the memory of the protestant Calas that Voltaire is regarded as the (noneponymous) hero of the "race of intellectuals," as one used to say at Altenburg (or at Pontigny). What's more, it is not in the least irrelevant that, well before the substantivization of the term "intellectuals," their position or function had been more or less contemporaneous with the transformation affecting the word "protestation" itself: *disapprobation, opposition, indignation, refusal*, etc., thus encompassing the Latin (and religious) meaning of attestation—of a belief, of a faith, of a conviction. Protestantism is seen as the symptom, if not the agent, of the collapse of the theologico-political. Intellectual protestation, on the other hand, stems initially from rebellion against religious totalitarianism.[39]

Against religious totalitarianism—that is to say, "against theologico-political substantialism (embodied sovereignty, from the Lord to the lord)."[40] Without contenting himself with opposing the revolt of Protestantism to the absolute of Judaism, Lacoue-Labarthe, at the end of his text, proposes defiance as an ethical task:

> Protestation is such that it implies a *defiance*—and I shall add: one that is final [*sans appel*]. Or, if one prefers: it implies a responsibility that responds to nothing (to no injunction), nor to anyone (to no plea), that does not even rely on the "one must [*il faut*]" that it nevertheless declares when it is confronted with the raw fact of injustice and evil—two "concepts that are rather difficult to 'determine.'"[41]

In being faithful to the exorbitant demand to free oneself from myth and to the difficulty it gives rise to, his wariness about the proposition "without myth" developing into a myth is linked to the attention paid by Lacoue-Labarthe to the transposition of dates in Blanchot's very last book—an attention that oscillates between the dubious element involved in a calculation ("a final calculation: that of the incalculable," as was argued in relation to the fragment) and an uncertain, perhaps failing calculation. This twofold stumbling block leads to an aporia, causing Lacoue-Labarthe's book to stall as the questions become so strenuous they reach a deadlock. An aporia or enigma, then, exposed in the clarity of the question of myth thus clarified and driven to an impasse.

In the same discussion that followed the delivery of "Fidelities" at Cerisy, Lacoue-Labarthe ventured to sketch out an ethics based on what Blanchot's manoeuvre [*opération*] itself seemed to call for:

> I felt a tremendous naivety because I said that I subscribed naively to "Freud and the Future." This text by Thomas Mann condenses quite a number of analyses that were being made in circles close to him and that he knew well, analyses by Kerényi or even earlier ones on what he calls "life in citation [*la vie en citation*]," that is to say, "life in myth."[42] One cannot distinguish here between citations made consciously from those made unconsciously, or citations that are in one's control from those that are not. I didn't mean to say that Blanchot was thinking of Rousseau or Montaigne when he wrote this text [*The Instant of My Death*], absolutely not; rather, that a memory of French literature—or in his case, of other literatures as well—is at work here, such that something of the order of citation [*quelque chose comme du citationnel*] can appear, I shall say, almost on the surface of the text.
>
> The other example is "A Primal Scene." [. . .] In *Faux pas*, there is a short article on William Blake's *The Marriage of Heaven and Hell* in which Blanchot makes a point of recalling that Blake had seen God at the window as a child.[43] When, thirty-five years on, he writes "A Primal Scene," he recounts the story of that child who sees that "nothing is what there is, and first of all nothing beyond." It is of that same citational order; it is something that belongs to what we call literature, that is, a kind of vast string or interweaving of sentences, but sentences that involve perhaps always just a few, extremely condensed, clustered, singular experiences—in fact, a very small, infinitesimal number of them, not to say one, single experience. One cannot make these kinds of distinctions; I think it would very quickly become untenable. And what's all the more strange in Blanchot's case is that he is a literary critic of immense culture, to say the least, and that one might have expected from him to cite with full knowledge of the facts. Nothing of the sort. [. . .]
>
> He writes "A Primal Scene"—a first version of it [. . .]; he then rewrites it, suspending the title and removing in the body of the text the word "primal" from the phrase "primal scene"; he then frames this in *The Writing of the Disaster* with a whole series of texts to say "it sounds all too fictional" [. . .];

and then he summons Ovid's myth of Narcissus and reflects upon the mythical element of that myth. It is apparent that Blanchot is fighting a battle, and in my view that's what constitutes the remarkable greatness of his last texts: he is fighting something he himself has undergone, what in fact I call, after Thomas Mann, "mythic citation," and he gets rid of it, he tries to get rid of it, perhaps even knowing that one cannot get rid of it. But knowing also that ethics would be precisely that: to cease citing. Or else to cite truly, but here I'd put it differently: to cite writings [*écritures*] truly—I'm not thinking of Scripture [*l'Écriture*] or that sort of thing but of the meticulousness that consists in working, as Benjamin imagined, by collecting quotations, by assembling quotations. That is perhaps the work we all do, but we don't declare it.

I'd prefer the word "declaration" to phrases like "with full knowledge of the facts"[44] or "in all conscience"; it seems to me to be more accurate: to declare citation. My first reaction was to regard *The Instant of My Death* as, quite simply, astonishing [*foudroyant*], and then I said to myself: "But after all, it is mythic and Blanchot doesn't get out of it." And then, because of the Malraux episode, I said to myself not: "he knows full well what he is doing" but: "there's this indication: the Malraux reference." One would have to work for hours on end on this debate with Malraux, which I think took place and which at times comes to the surface very explicitly and at other times remains secret. Malraux's name means: I declare that I'm trying not to cite any longer. Yet at the very moment in which he declares: "I'm trying not to cite any longer," he is still citing. But it is perhaps the only gesture that allows us to come closest, asymptotically, to what might be something like a moral law, which would consist in saying: I abstain from citation; no more figures, no more models, no more examples, no more representations that guide our actions. Instead, let us try to follow a course of action that is removed from all reference. Which is, of course—and this I believe deeply, or else there would be no moral difficulties nor evil—the impossible itself.

★

One could stop here, at this injunction, which in many ways is unsurpassable. This is the edge reached by Lacoue-Labarthe's book, which at the same time timidly but unmistakably also indicates the next step. The above declaration already sketches it out: it entails comparing *The Instant of My Death*—and the kind of "manoeuvre [*opération*]" performed there by Blanchot around the gesture that consists in signaling Malraux and the shift in dates—and the manoeuvre that involves endlessly returning to, requestioning, and reinterpreting "A Primal Scene." Although the book breaks off here, Lacoue-Labarthe, in a series of six seminars—under the title "L'instance de la mort"[45]—obstinately continued to engage with *The Writing of the Disaster*, running counter to its fragmentation and paying careful, meticulous attention to the cuts and displacements applied to previously published texts. So as to reopen rather than conclude this discussion, we would like to indicate briefly the avenues explored by these seminars.

In these seminars, Lacoue-Labarthe puts *The Instant of My Death* to the test of a number of rifts that chart *The Writing of the Disaster*, in particular all the sequences organized by "a very explicit, almost brutal, and apparently irrevocable challenge to those two motifs" essential to *The Instant of My Death*—that is, autobiography and etymology. For example, Blanchot's entire book wrestles with the role played by the word "disaster," inevitably marked by its etymon, whereas, fourteen years later, *The Instant of My Death* overstresses the "instance" looming over the word "instant." With this series of paradoxes in mind, Lacoue-Labarthe attempts to take a step further by elaborating two motifs that open up the possibility of interpreting the manoeuvre risked by Blanchot. With regard to the first motif, he coins the phrase "amnesic patience," and as for the second motif, he takes up the dialogue inaugurated by "Dismay" on the question of the secret.[46]

In discussing "amnesic patience," Lacoue-Labarthe highlights in Blanchot the precarious state of an exit—neither passive nor decisive (unlike the decision of existence in Heidegger or the will of oblivion in Nietzsche)—from myth, from life in myth or from life in citation. In the wake of Blanchot, this "amnesic patience" would thus be a kind of watchword for the impossible ethical task he had glimpsed during the discussion at Cerisy. The said phrase was formed by drawing directly on "Discours sur la patience"[47] (a text reworked and redistributed in fragments in *The Writing of the Disaster*), that is, Blanchot's dialogue with Emmanuel Levinas, which goes back to *Awaiting Oblivion*. More directly still, however, the phrase was made possible thanks to a letter Blanchot had sent to Laporte on September 24, 1966, which contained a kind of "preview" of "A Primal Scene," described there as a "memory [. . .] at the center of oblivion." Returning to the narrative that recounts the scene he confides to Laporte, Blanchot added: "Naturally, such an impulse proves nothing, uncovers nothing: that would be the last straw. But at least this joy of extraordinary purity, the memory of which is at the center of oblivion, has in a sense revealed to me a level of 'myself,' a demand on which I later had occasion to reflect by trying to respond to it."

The opening of the third seminar, delivered on April 15, 2005, reads as follows:

If, drawing on brief remarks regarding the rather fierce battle Blanchot wages against etymologism (in fact, in *The Instant of My Death* he himself plays on the words instant/instance, in the same way as in *The Writing of the Disaster* a kind of extraordinary memory of language has him oscillate between words that he knows full well are related and have their "own" meaning), if one could—and this is precisely the question that needs to be asked—place Blanchot's thought or writing under the sign or emblem of a figure, it would obviously be that of Mnemosyne, the mother of the Muses. That is to say, essentially and inseparably, music and poetry—according to the most anciently attested tradition, also taken up by Pindar. [. . .] Based on that and it being understood that all of Blanchot's obstinate determination from the period of *The Space of Literature* onward (the mid-1950s), all of his efforts amount to dis-figuring [*dé-figurer*], to de-mythologizing [*dé-mythologiser*] his thought—that is, to making sure that no figure (no type) would be capable of emblematizing his approach or what he has long referred to as "the essence of writing" (a negative, which the figure of Mnemosyne would emblematize)—one could speak of what I venture to call "Blanchot's amnesic patience."

Amnesia is a pathology that amounts to the destruction of memory. The word is perhaps too negative, but I have in mind the kind of undermining, ruining, or destroying practiced by Blanchot, first vis-à-vis what is referred to, in the medical field, as hypermnesia (see Blanchot's text devoted to Louis-René des Forêts' *The Bavard*, where he speaks very powerfully of "a demented memory"), and second, vis-à-vis that which, since Plato, has been the very impetus [*ressort*] of philosophical thought, namely anamnesis, the memorial ascent [*remontée mémoriale*] into that which—and this is what must be acknowledged as the power of Plato's thought, which has never weakened, despite all the reversals—has, after all, never been present (ideas, etc.).

In these two texts by Blanchot ("A Primal Scene," *The Instant of My Death*), in these narrative mementos, these fragments of memory, mnemonic *but* haunted by "amnesic patience," one finds, in spite of everything, a final, perhaps very weakened, expiring echo of that myth of Orpheus out of which Blanchot had made the myth of literature itself: the crossing of the river of oblivion, Lethe, in order to return, assuming such an undertaking could succeed, with the truth, that is, the *aletheia*, according to Heidegger's etymology. Even though Blanchot was suspicious of this myth and kept it at bay, he continued, in his correspondence, to quote "that shallow, calumniated stream: death" (Mallarmé).[48]

The seminar lists three "mnemic or memory instances in relation to which Blanchot practices his amnesic patience": *the instance of language* or of the memory of language, that is, the imposition of language, its precedence, which coincides with that of death; *the instance of literature*, that is, "the absolute anteriority of narrative, of invocation or incantation over all possible discourses"; *the instance of memory*, understood as a faculty itself, which haunts modern literature. Lacoue-Labarthe concludes:

> Writing, in that sense, would be to attempt to win out over the imposition of these three instances, over this triple authority, which means that, in truth, we are, on all three counts, dictated (this is a language I'm in the habit of using, take it for what it's worth). We are in the grip of a text that we hear but that is forever untranscribable—*Wir sind gedichtet*. This is what makes Blanchot say that "'I' am dead before being born."

Consequently, one can see how the said amnesic patience, in close proximity to what Blanchot called, apropos Simone Weil, "mythic transposition," opens up, eroding the latter, a different perspective onto the confusion of dates in the narrative. In the notes left for "Crypteia," a missing chapter of this book, one comes across the following phrase: "strictly anachronistic anniversary." On that basis, couldn't this be seen as a way of outplaying chronological fiction itself, a way of paradoxically declaring citation? In fact, patient-amnesic existence (not to say "the work" of this amnesic patience, which precisely does not work as such, does not produce work) ends up appearing in the very partition of the present book, as is apparent through the subtitles of the book's two sections, neutralized as it were by the very scheme Blanchot had applied to the title of "A Primal Scene," the latter having been withdrawn in parentheses and inflected by a question mark: "(20 July?)," "(22 September?)."

The amnesic patience, which designates the very task of writing as well as, at bottom, that of existence, allows for the worry or at least the question of the secret, already formulated in "Dismay," to resurface. What meaning can Blanchot's phrase "Henceforth he will live in the secret" still have if what is at stake is precisely to free oneself from all recourse to references, that is, to the possibility of a reserve? And this affects the possibility of speaking [*la possibilité du dire*] as much as it does the presence of the world: "nothing is what there is, and first of all nothing beyond"—which not only presents itself for all to see but disrupts everything. To Lacoue-Labarthe's remark in "Dismay": "*there is no secret, but that remains unavowable*," Blanchot replies in *The Writing of the Disaster*, as a long dialogue unfolds around the fate of Western thought—which is to penetrate the secret of nature—combining the voices of Nietzsche, Heidegger, Levinas, Bataille, and Klossowski (to mention only those who are easily identifiable): "*The secret alluded to is that there is none, except for those who refuse avowal.*"[49] Lacoue-Labarthe provides the following commentary:

> Blanchot speaks of a secret that is limitless, as it were, that cannot be penetrated: there is no unveiling of what there is in the celebrated withdrawal of being, "the obscurity of the clearing"—which is what Heidegger says in his own way. The secret: what is hidden in the crypt is the necessity of the crypt. The secret is the crypt of a crypt, and this twice-hidden being amounts to not being hidden at all: there is no secret (there is no secret content), and, if there is no secret, the enigma (again Heraclitus) continues to govern, and so there is no rest [*c'est le non-repos*]. [. . .] Like a kind of avowal: perhaps there is no secret at all in "A Primal Scene." A certain reading [. . .], based on that sentence about the secret, bothered Blanchot, whose response carries with it the entire fate of language and the entire fate of ontology.

Less than two years later, in his last text, Lacoue-Labarthe, for his part, ventured to cite the primal scene of the very unveiling of that which appears [*le paraître*]. The said text, or rather sketch, entitled "Postface," would be added to "La disparition," a remarkable narrative about a dream (that of the death of its author) written forty years earlier. Shortly before his death, Lacoue-Labarthe was anxious to have this narrative preceded by two extracts drawn from Blanchot.[50] We shall end here, with this final quotation, leaving it resonate with everything that haunts the incompletion of *Ending and Unending Agony*:

> Twice, then, I have died. In the space of barely a few months: May 25, 2006, December 29 of the same year. Each time, thanks to powerful means, I was brought back to consciousness—as the expression goes—that is, to this world in its entirety, this world that *is* because it *appears*, without the slightest exception. But each time, I had the fleeting intuition that what presented itself as the world was above all that it *existed* (*that* it was present), of an existence that imperceptibly preceded the full existence of everything.
>
> Such was the underside of disappearance. An effacement of the condition of existing—that pure impossibility. In short, furtively, the impossible had become possible for me (". . . a flash of lightning, then the night . . ."); and at that sign, I suddenly recognized the condition of poetic existence. Which is not to pass through appearances (precisely, there are no appearances) but to risk standing at the place [point] of origin of that which appears, which is everything. Metaphysical funambulism without metaphysical safeguards. Or, if one prefers: *emptied* metaphysical experience, pure exposure to nothingness [in the very movement of its absolute withdrawal].[51]

Prologue

In one of his *Fictions*, "The Secret Miracle," Borges imagines the strange death of a writer from Prague—"author of the uncompleted tragedy *The Enemies*, of a *Defence of Eternity*, and of a study of Jakob Boehme's indirect Jewish sources"[1]—who is arrested by the Gestapo in March 1939 and sentenced to be shot by firing squad under the sole pretext of being Jewish and denounced as such. The night preceding his execution, he dreams that the very voice of God (clear and distinct, and truthful, according to Maimonides, because the speaker is invisible) grants him the time needed to complete his work. The following day at dawn, "when the time comes [*au moment voulu*]," that is, between the moment in which the soldiers of the firing squad point their rifles at him, as the hand of the officer goes up to give the order to open fire (to carry out the sentence, "the death sentence [*l'arrêt de mort*]"), and the moment in which the deadly shot goes off—in that very brief but tremendously long, almost eternal *instant*[2]—the time of the "physical universe" is suspended, as it were, and the writer reworks and brings the text, written in hexameters, of the final act of his play to completion: he completes his "work" in secret, even though it remains forever unfinished.

When considered from the viewpoint of his last published "narrative [*récit*]," *The Instant of My Death* (1994), and of an earlier enigmatic "autobiographical" fragment, of which there are at least two versions—it appears under its definitive title, "(A Primal Scene?)," in *The Writing of the Disaster* (1980)—one has perhaps every right to consider Borges's tale as being quite emblematic of Blanchot's "unworked" *work* [œuvre "*désœuvrée*"]. A work entirely written or rewritten, completed yet uncompletable, within the incommensurable time that separates July 20, 1944—the date on which he was very nearly shot dead by the Nazis (or some other day, in the winter of 1914 or 1915, when he experienced a childhood ecstasy)—from his death, which has now taken place on February 20, 2003: the timeless time of originary agony [*agonie native*] and immemorial death, of "necessary impossible" death, which will have *authorized* the last meditation of he who had relentlessly explored Literature or Writing in its very possibility.

The two parts that make up the present book, which are themselves divided—not to say "fragmented"—in various more or less brief essays, attempt to propose a reading of these two texts. More precisely, they question them: not to lay suspicion upon them but to put to the test that which, through the haunting of "dying" [*la hantise du "mourir"*], has come into play with regard to the major categories of fiction and myth, of the testimonial and the testamentary, of the avowal and the secret, of non-self-presence [*non-présence à soi*] and withdrawal, of the (ethical) other and (political) being-together, etc., but especially with regard to what we must resign ourselves to calling Blanchot's *posthumous writing*.

The first part, unsurprisingly, borrows its title from Borges: "The Secret Miracle." Owing to multiple allusions (to Goya and Büchner, to Malraux and Bataille, but also to Montaigne and Rousseau, as well as to a few others) which are gradually elucidated, it is subtitled: "(20 July?)." The title of the second part, eventually extended to the book as a whole: "Ending and Unending Agony," draws syntactically on the title of a well-known essay by Freud devoted to psychoanalysis;[3] the word "agony," on the other hand, comes from the terminology used by Winnicott, whom Blanchot had read carefully at a time when, in line with "A Primal Scene," he wrote a commentary on Serge Leclaire's book *A Child Is Being Killed*. The subtitle—again a date: "(22 September?)"—recalls the day of Blanchot's "death-birth," in 1907, but also the night, which Blanchot has often mentioned, when Kafka made his entrance into literature by writing *The Verdict* in one stretch on September 23, 1912. Celan, whom Blanchot regarded as "the last to speak,"[4] claimed that Poetry is "the memory of dates."[5]

1
"The Secret Miracle" (20 July?)

Fidelities

My dear Jacques,

I had sworn not to give in to it, to do everything in my power to avoid it, and not to allow myself to be drawn in. A sentence, slightly overemphatic, but obstinately recurring, put it plainly to me: I don't want to succumb; I don't want this endless return of the same *demons*; I don't want this kind of "eternal repetition [*ressassement éternel*]."[1]

Before long, however, I realized that it was impossible. Strictly impossible.

Then, another sentence, just as emphatic, I'm afraid, began to voice itself in me: I'll yield to autobiography; I'll make that sacrifice. And when I understood that eventually, in order to make a start, I would have to utter this sentence publicly, it immediately seemed clear to me that the right course to follow was simply to let the formidable phrase that had thus come to the fore echo in all its harmonic depth: I'll make that sacrifice [*j'y sacrifierai*]. And leave it at that.

I think—I know—that you all will understand. And you, Jacques, first and foremost.

In the autumn of 1994, you and I, among others no doubt, received this very short, extraordinary, and deeply moving "narrative" by Maurice Blanchot: *The Instant of My Death*. For reasons that are of course very different (I'm certainly not making any comparisons) but that are perhaps at bottom not so unrelated through some secret or tacit affinity, I know, or I think I know, that this text touched us not merely because we couldn't but take it to be Maurice Blanchot's "last will and testament," as difficult as that might be to say or to think—the last pages that he had the strength to write and that, in a final gesture, he was anxious to bequeath and address—but also because we immediately considered it to be one of the most admirable literary texts of our time (I'm deliberately avoiding the terms "modern" or "contemporary"), perhaps one of the most beautiful pieces of "prose" in all of French literature, if not one of the most sublime—*stricto sensu*—"narratives" ever written.

I know, moreover, or I think I know, that this dismay [*émoi*]—something entirely different from an emotion—was so great and powerful that both of us (but we were not alone), without of course conferring with each other, had decided there and then, in the place to which our task or profession had assigned us, to interrupt the course of our teaching and devote, exceptionally, several hours to reading this text. (If I know, or think I know, this to be the case, it is because an Italian student, who at the time was attending your seminar on testimony and had come to visit a friend of his in Strasbourg—who, in turn, was one of my students—attended the session at which I attempted my first commentary on *The Instant of My Death*. At the end of the session, he came to see me and told me how very strange it all was: two days earlier, that very week—it must have been in November, if I recall correctly—he had heard your own commentary. And because he noticed at once that I knew nothing about this and saw my bewilderment, he himself was surprised, though very tactfully so, by what was in his eyes such a remarkable coincidence. In fact, later on, it was he who, perhaps out of the same tactfulness, sent me a copy of the Italian translation of your text, published in *Aut aut*, which I sought to decipher as best I could before being able to read—and reread—*Demeure*.[2] In French, that is. . . .)

My first reading—an impromptu reading, in the wake of dismay—was manifestly insufficient. I know it all too well. Then, stricken with remorse and as irresistibly fascinated as I was on the first day by the abyssal limpidity of this text, I set to work again in the rather vain hope of doing better—or less badly. The first time, all too briefly (and without having read your own text), at a seminar held in Jerusalem in the spring of 1996. Then a second time this year, during a whole semester devoted to "philosophical autobiography." This time I had read—and reread—your text, and because I had the time, I combined my reading with my commentary on the two versions of "A Primal Scene" (that enigmatic autobiographical prose poem) and on all the difficult, complex texts and fragments in *The Writing of the Disaster* that, between disquiet and repentance [*repentir*], circumscribe the modified, reworked version [*la reprise modifiée*] and that, at the cost of the twofold suspension of the title,[3] question vertiginously the categories of the scene and of the secret, of primitiveness, of fiction, even of myth. This has been a longstanding project of mine since the publication of *The Writing of the Disaster* in 1980, one I had never been able to carry out and to which, unfortunately, I cannot return today.

I will limit myself, then, to *The Instant of My Death*.

On the occasion that gathers us here, on the eve of your birthday and in accordance with what is, I admit, the strange law of my fidelities (since such is the title that I had blindly chosen and that I have kept), I would simply like to bear witness, as a kind of present to you, to the passion that we have shared and that brought us, far from one another, close together (the law of my fidelities is that of e-strangement [*é-loignement*]—I know that you know this and know it better than I do, and I'm also thinking of the initial address of "A Primal Scene"), around these pages from "a heart that beats no more"[4] and in which we recognized what haunts us: literature.

I won't set my reading in opposition to your own, which, on the contrary, I will assume throughout everyone knows well. In any case, I have nothing to say "in opposition" to you and certainly nothing that would be "my own interpretation." Nor will I submit anything for you to judge or evaluate: you have already been doing that for ten years at least, I'm proud to say. I will simply tell you what I have done or tried to do, and this won't even mean my addressing one or more questions to you. I will just confide in you what is closest to my heart: the part of me that pertains to what I call, in my earliest language, my demon.

To clarify matters, I must recall briefly the circumstances of that autumn of 1994.

I was teaching a class on negativity. The class was in principle intended for second-year students (it was therefore a kind of "introductory course," to "contemporary thought," in this case), but as usual, the audience was quite heterogeneous, and as usual, I had to switch registers constantly, which is both difficult and exhausting. My intention—an unfeasible one, as I knew full well, and I was already counting on the following year—was to show:

1. That the transcendental problematic amounts to the rigorously onto-logical formalization of the question of the origin as Rousseau had uneasily but firmly elaborated it with respect to the relationship between nature and art (*physis* and *techne*), that is, as a radical reinterpretation of the Aristotelian concept of *mimesis*. From this perspective, it was no accident that Kant, for example, spoke of schematism as "an art concealed within the depths of the human soul";[5]

2. That the dialectical-speculative onto-logic was tenable only by virtue of having understood the (transcendental) *condition* as the necessity of mediateness and negativity. To illustrate my argument—and not betray the voice or injunction of my mimetological demon—I turned to the three matrix "scenes" of speculative metaphysics, that is, the three great exemplary interpretations of tragedy put forward between 1795 and 1804: that of *Oedipus* by Schelling (in the *Letters on Dogmatism and Criticism*), that of *Antigone* by Hölderlin (in the *Remarks*: "God present in the figure of death"),[6] and that

of the *Eumenides* by Hegel (in the article on natural law: "this is the eternal tragedy that the Absolute enacts with itself").[7] This was so until the theological model in the *Phenomenology of Spirit* imposed itself—a model derived from Luther that already secretly governed all these interpretations of tragedy: "the harsh words of Luther: God himself is dead";[8]

3. That the question of negativity was consequently the question of death as the in-finitely paradoxical (infinitely "impossible") condition of possibility of life, or rather—but Heidegger was still my distant horizon that year, and how does one compromise on what is nothing like a "nuance"?—of *existence*.

Having reached this point, and in order to take a break and give students a text to read, I handed out copies of Bataille's well-known article "Hegel, Death, and Sacrifice"—a text on which you yourself have written a memorable commentary and that, I have to confess, hasn't left my side since my student days (I still use my old copy of issue number 5 of *Deucalion*, bought in 1963 . . .). I thus had students comment on Kojève's formulation that mankind is "death living a human life," which for Kojève accounts for the fact that "Hegel's 'dialectical' or anthropological philosophy is in the final analysis a *philosophy of death* (or of atheism, which amounts to the same thing)."[9] I then had them consider the paragraphs in which Bataille introduces the motif of comedy ("The Tragi-comic Aspect of Mankind's Divinity"; "The death of Jesus partakes of comedy"; etc.),[10] but in which, having recalled the page—of "capital importance"—in the preface of the *Phenomenology* regarding "the life of Spirit," which "is not the life that shies away from death,"[11] etc., he comes to the question of sacrifice, which obviously does more and better than anticipate and is so closely related to what Blanchot would later call "experience without experience" or the "unexperienced experience" of death.[12]

All of you here know this analysis—which, incidentally, stems from what is in my view an implacable question: Is it Hegel who articulates the truth of sacrifice, or is it sacrifice (this "practically universal institution")[13] that holds the secret of Hegel's philosophy?

I will single out just these two passages (it is no doubt a weakness of mine to believe that we don't pay enough attention to them):

> For when the animal being supporting him dies, the human being himself ceases to be. In order for mankind to reveal itself ultimately to itself, it would have to die, but it would have to do it while living—watching itself ceasing to be. In other words, death itself would have to become (self-)consciousness at the very moment that it annihilates the conscious being. In a sense, this is what takes place (what at least is on the verge of taking place, or which takes place

> in a fugitive, ungraspable manner) by means of a subterfuge. In the sacrifice, the sacrificer identifies himself with the animal that is struck down dead. And so he dies in seeing himself die, and even, in a certain way, by his own will, one in spirit with the sacrificial weapon. But it is a comedy!
>
> At least it would be a comedy if some other method existed which could reveal to the living the invasion of death.
>
> [. . .]
>
> This difficulty proclaims the necessity of *spectacle*, or of *representation* in general, without the practice of which it would be possible for us to remain alien and ignorant vis-à-vis death, just as beasts apparently are. Indeed, nothing is less animal than fiction, which is more or less separated from the real, from death.
>
> Mankind does not live by bread alone, but also by the comedies with which it willingly deceives itself. In mankind it is the animal, it is the natural being, that eats. But mankind takes part in rites and spectacles. Or else it can read: and so literature prolongs in it—inasmuch as it is sovereign, authentic literature—the haunting magic of spectacles, tragic or comic.
>
> It is a question, in tragedy at least, of our identifying with some character who dies, and of believing that we die although we are alive. Furthermore, pure and simple imagination suffices, but it has the same meaning as the classic subterfuges, spectacles, or books, to which the masses have recourse.*

That is as far as I had got.

To be fair, I should add that right around that time, at the request of the Théâtre national de Strasbourg, which wished to honor the "reading" of Artaud's well-known Vieux-Colombier lecture (delivered in 1947), to be staged by Philippe Clévenot (a remarkable actor to whom I'm bound by an e-strangement for over twenty years), I had written two short pages that I had entitled "Birth Is Death,"[14] and that, after having hesitated between several propositions by Novalis, I had placed under the sign of the last verse of Hölderlin's "reconstituted" poem "In lovely blueness . . .": "Living is a death, and death is also a life."[15] (I had dedicated this text "To the memory of Sarah,"[16] and today, I feel a pang when I think that at the time Jean-Luc[17] had wanted for us to set off again from there and thus continue our interrupted conversation, our "Scene," and I still retain the hope—an immeasurable hope—that, yes, we will continue our conversation.)

* Georges Bataille, "Hegel, Death, and Sacrifice," trans. Jonathan Strauss, *Yale French Studies* 78 (1990): 19–20; Georges Bataille, "Hegel, la mort et le sacrifice" (1955), in *Œuvres complètes* (Paris: Gallimard, 1988), 12:336–337.

In that piece, I proposed, somewhat hastily or rashly, the following hypothesis: that two matrix scenes, or two "primal scenes" (to revert to the terminology I used at the time), could be said to preside over the West and its literature. Or the West as literature. And both scenes stem from the Homeric poems.

The scene of *wrath*, set up by the *Iliad*: *menin aeide thea*,[18] which, besides, is not just the scene of protestation and revolt, as is known, but also that of thought and memory, as can be seen so powerfully in Marx's early writings, for example.

And the scene of *experience*—if one recalls the original maritime sense of the term, the truth of which is illuminated at the very center of the *Odyssey* in the famous *nekyia*, that is, Ulysses's descent to hell, his journey through death.

I'm not far from thinking, like Bataille, that these two scenes respond to "practically universal institutions" (this is at any rate undoubtedly the case for the second scene, which is found in all rites of initiation or of legitimation of sovereignty), and you'll perhaps recall that I'm feeble or naïve enough to believe in the aptness of the remarkable demonstration presented by Thomas Mann to Freud for his eightieth birthday in 1936 (a date belonging to the fascist era of our time) on "life in myth" as "life in citations"[19]—that is, *imitatio*, if you will, and sacred repetition, from which nothing less than the following can be inferred: that the sacred, religion in the sense of *re-legere*, could be said to be *repetition* itself. (Thomas Mann's lecture is entitled "Freud and the Future," and it appears in the French edition of his selected writings, published under the title *Noblesse de l'esprit*.) From this perspective, our historical deeds, as well as our so-called daily existence, cannot escape this compulsive law any more than literature can—to say nothing, precisely, of the unconscious.

It is not too difficult to see that between the vehemence of *To Have Done with the Judgment of God*, for example, and the (twofold) account he gives of his own death (at Rodez and on Golgotha) in the "Vieux-Colombier Lecture," Artaud almost meticulously reenacts—or cites—these two scenes. Nor is it so difficult to see with what precision these two scenes come together in *The Instant of My Death*, where protestation (albeit scarcely wrathful, on the face of it) against injustice combines with the stupefying elation of the infinitely paradoxical experience of death.

That, then, is as far as I had got.

And I undertook to write a commentary on this text, or, quite simply, to read it. I thought this was absolutely necessary and involved, I believe, a necessity unlike any I had ever felt before.

I had little difficulty with the anecdote itself (if I may venture such a word): for a long time, I had known, albeit indirectly, of the existence of this episode (another word I hardly dare use, given how strongly I had sensed Blanchot's reservations about it), and I had even learned, of late, when and where it happened.* I even believed, ingenuously, that I could account for certain contingent facts of the narrative that at first sight might be considered rather surprising. The Nazi lieutenant, for example, who expressed himself in "shamefully normal French"[20] and whose troops were made up of Russians of the Vlasov army was quite simply a French SS, of which there were many, and a civil war was brewing beneath the international war referred to in a brief paragraph on the first page, or was accommodating the class warfare that, as ever, sanctions the injustices of war. I could also at that time provide essential details concerning "Blanchot's political itinerary," as it is called, about which so many foul or idiotic "revelations" or "exegeses" have been or are still being smugly divulged, thereby testifying to the fact that we have in effect still not done with fascism. Moreover, I was aware of the error in the date regarding the Jena events in the autumn of 1806: the victorious and brutal occupation by French troops; the world's soul "concentrated" on his horse;[21] Hegel protecting, under his coat (it was raining), the manuscript of the preface to his great Book (he had gone out to post it, that is, to save it)—a book that was so indispensable to Bataille's and Blanchot's thinking and that could just as well be entitled the *Autothanatography of Spirit*. Just as Blanchot in July 1994 wrote *The Instant of My Death* almost fifty years to the day after the event recounted therein, in the same way, he was able obscurely to dream or think that, his own birth date coinciding with the centenary of the founding of his family home, he was in a sense born of that era when, as Europe was decisively entering the age of "philosophical wars" (as Nietzsche put it), this terrible sentence was written and saved—terrible because it was still terribly comforting and archaic, thus testifying, in spite of everything, to an ancient faith: "But the life of Spirit is not the life that shies away from death." And that perhaps explains why, at the heart of the narrative, the scene of the Passion is also cited, as the art of representation in the Christian West has for centuries depicted it: the "almost priestly" gait of the young man, the procession of women (the same ones, or very nearly so, as those who, at the foot of the Cross, performed the Deposition of Christ in the Lamentation),[22]

* Since the publication of Christophe Bident's "biographical essay," it has become clear that Blanchot's attribution of dates in this text is far from precise, let alone "reliable." The stakes here are decisive. I'll return to this later. See Christophe Bident, *Maurice Blanchot. Partenaire invisible* (Seyssel: Champ Vallon, 1998), esp. 228–232, 581–583.

and the very words of eschatology: "It is finished"—in the mode, of course, of the "as if,"[23] that is to say, precisely, of *imitatio*.

The text's limpidity, as I said, is not misleading; it is abyssal. The clarity of the writing is its very enigma. I have had much difficulty, I confess, on the three occasions I ventured to do this in an academic context (irrespective of my audience), in awakening even an inkling of sensitivity to the sober beauty of its phrasing—which, one has to admit, is completely and utterly French. Quite simply, how can one get anyone to appreciate the following, which is magnificent: "At that instant—an abrupt return to the world—the considerable noise of a nearby battle broke out [*À cet instant, brusque retour au monde, éclata le bruit considérable d'une proche bataille*]."[24] The one thing that kept me going had been given to me by the person who is closest to me—and the most e-stranged [*é-loigné*]—and through whom I'm bound, for almost thirty years now, to the date of a certain July 20. (I know, I know, Freud, who was himself prone to the superstition of dates, pointed the finger of suspicion at this most archaic form of autobiographical compulsion and its commemorative rituals.) It is a sentence by La Motte that Louis Racine quotes in the memoirs he wrote on his father. It seemed to me to go right to the heart of the matter: "What he invented seemed to be missing from language, rather than violating it."[25]

As for the narrative's protocol, finally, as for the thoughts articulated therein [*énoncés de pensée*] (if one can call them that), I have tried, like you, albeit within my own capabilities (and without addressing the vast question of testimony that underlies your argument), to provide explanations. Not *since* I had to, but *because* I had to: this is the categorical injunction of any text of this magnitude. I recalled *Death Sentence* and *The Step Not Beyond* (and of course your own analyses, which I'll have the modesty not to describe); in *The Writing of the Disaster*, I singled out everything that might be summoned under the heading of autobiography and biography (of the writer, as exemplified by the following paraphrase of Heidegger: "He died, he lived, he died"),[26] of immemorial and always anterior or, as it were, originary death ("You are dead already"),[27] of the endless debate with the dialectic, etc.; I also worked on the notions of the instant and of insistence (as well as of "desistance" [*désistance*],[28] which I learned from you and for which I can never thank you enough), and on the question of the *instance*, in every sense of the word (temporal, topographical, juridical, linguistic: the theory of pronouns, the passage from "I" to "He," which for Blanchot signals the entrance into literature, and to "You," which also marks a passage, but to what, to whom . . . ?); I recalled, furthermore, the necessarily autothanatographical character of any autobiography, which applies to the entirety of its tradition, at least since Augustine's *Confessions* (which are also yours) and for their mystical legacy, as exemplified, closer to our time—that is, since the invention of literature—by the *Memoirs from Beyond the Grave* or *A Season in Hell*; I even mentioned *The Practice of Joy Before Death*, wondering about the very absence of this word, which Bataille had so obviously borrowed from John of the Cross and Teresa of Ávila (or even from Pascal and Nietzsche), in the otherwise heavily mystical language that Blanchot uses, not without thinking of Bataille: beatitude, sovereign elation, happiness, ecstasy. (I think I can say here that I owe the opportunity of having been able to consult Blanchot's manuscript to the affectionate friendship of Jacqueline Laporte, who transcribed it for the publisher—more than ever do I yield here to autobiography, thus making another sacrifice, and I didn't utter the word "friendship" by accident. There are very few corrections or words crossed out; it is all written in one single stroke, or very nearly so. The only passage where Blanchot was truly hesitant, as we say, is the one on page 5 [11], which is also where the following vocabulary finds its way, as we say again, into his language: he hesitated over the order of appearance of the words "beatitude," "elation," "immortal," and "eternal" and over the phrase "mortal elation," just after the question with which Bataille's very voice resonates: "—sovereign elation?" which he finally crossed out, leaving instead just the following sentence, which is yet another question: "The encounter of death with death?")

Naturally, I made no pretence of being exhaustive in my reading. I had scarcely skimmed through these few pages before I knew that they required nothing less than a kind of infinite commentary. It wasn't just the vanishing line of Blanchot's entire oeuvre and the rustling therein of the whole of literature—to say nothing of the commentaries it had already generated (beginning with your own) and of the dialogues in which it was engaged or that it prompted (nearby or far away, nearby and far away: how many names would have to be mentioned? They are probably all there, tacitly uttered, summoned, or recalled). Nor were there just those (always conceivable) sudden openings, with a mere word, onto vast questions (the proletariat or the nation, as Malraux would say, modern warfare and the theory of the partisan, as you remind us, the history of Europe since the collapse of the theologico-political, state terrorism, the arch-ethics of justice, etc.). Nor, even, was there simply Blanchot's own strategy—you yourself mention, with the greatest probity, the extent to which it is "calculated"—in relation to his political passion or obsession [*hantise*], of which he was clearly seeking to disclose the final meaning (in more satisfactory fashion than in the kind of "Memorandum" he entrusted to Roger Laporte in 1984).[29] There was above all the sense that within the transparency and the voiceless—or so distant—murmur of this narrative, within its almost speechless clarity (if one can still call it that), the dim but nonetheless audible and perceptible echo of an inexhaustible memory of language and of thought was lurking.

There remained only, glaring and resistant to my lack of resistance, the mention, on the deliberately detached penultimate page (the manuscript does indeed have "a blank space"), of Malraux's name (but also that of Paulhan, who gave the *NRF*[30] its "Résistance" credentials: I'll have a few words to say about this in a moment), and this paragraph, which seems "anecdotal" and sounds like a banal, romantic episode of a "return to ordinary life" (or, all things being equal, like the end of *Sentimental Education* or of a disillusioned *Bildungsroman*)—before the exhausted voice utters the very last words, which are vertiginous and which open onto the void of being brought to an eternal stand [*le vide de l'instance éternelle*].

Allow me to reread the paragraph in question:

> Later, having returned to Paris, he met Malraux. The latter told him that he had been taken prisoner (without being recognized) and that he had succeeded in escaping, losing a manuscript in the process. "It was only reflections on art, easy to reconstitute, whereas a manuscript would not be." With Paulhan, he made enquiries which could only remain vain.*

Why, then, Malraux? Why this business about a lost or confiscated manuscript? Why this narrative within a narrative? Or apparently so?

Ever since my years in secondary school and the awakening of my first literary passion (it was in fact Malraux), and ever since reading Gaëtan Picon's little (and in truth unequaled) book, which Malraux himself had annotated with stunning remarks that dazzled me, I know at least two things that, to my knowledge, have never been refuted, whatever the precautions that were taken vis-à-vis his mythomania:†

1. Wounded and arrested on July 22, 1944, near Gramat, in the Lot *dépar-*

* Maurice Blanchot, *The Instant of My Death*, trans. Elizabeth Rottenberg (Stanford, Calif.: Stanford University Press, 2000), 11; Maurice Blanchot, *L'instant de ma mort* (1994; Paris: Gallimard, 2002), 17.

† On this point, one should nonetheless consult the critical apparatus put together by Marius-François Guyard in the *Œuvres complètes* edition of the Bibliothèque de la Pléiade series (Paris: Gallimard, 1996), especially vol. 2 (which includes *Les noyers de l'Altenburg*) and vol. 3 (which includes, in *Le miroir des limbes*, the final version of the *Antimémoires*), where Malraux's "fabrications" are carefully listed.

tement, during a skirmish with units of the "Das Reich" Division, Malraux—under the name of Berger, the "Alsatian" name of the hero of *The Walnut Trees of Altenburg*, which can be pronounced equally well in German or French (Colonel Berger, then, of the Alsace-Lorraine Brigade)—was interrogated by the Gestapo and was subjected to a mock execution, just like Dostoyevsky, as he didn't fail to remind his readers, but also like so many others at the time, including Blanchot two days earlier, at the other end of France—a fact, it seems, of which he was not aware.*

2. Right around the same time (though one should be able to verify the exact date), during a house search, the Gestapo or the Milice confiscated, among other papers and documents, the manuscript of the second part of *The Struggle with the Angel*, of which the first part had been published in Lausanne in 1943 under that title and which Gallimard reprinted, this time under the definitive title of *The Walnut Trees of Altenburg*, with this explicit introductory note: "The remainder of *The Struggle with the Angel* was destroyed by the Gestapo. One can scarcely rewrite a novel," etc.† That was in 1948—in other words, the very year in which Blanchot's *Death Sentence* was first published. And if I highlight this coincidence, it is not without thinking of the equally strange fate of that book (Pierre Madaule talks about this) nor without harboring the rather vague and perhaps absurd or insignificant suspicion that this, in a first draft, was the "manuscript" that the Nazi lieutenant is said to have mistaken for "war plans."

"What does it matter,"[31] as Blanchot promptly adds. Indeed. But if we know nothing of what that second part of *The Struggle with the Angel* might have been, it is nevertheless very difficult to mistake *The Walnut Trees of Altenburg* for mere "reflections on art, easy to reconstitute." All the more so because in its last chapter or epilogue, *The Walnut Trees of Altenburg* contains one of the most powerful repetitions of the matrix *nekyia* I mentioned, the power of which, in my view, is further strengthened by the very fact that it is acknowledged as such in a kind of fervent stupefaction that only the

* The scene is recounted in André Malraux, *Antimemoirs*, trans. Terence Kilmartin (London: Hamish Hamilton, 1968), 154–184; André Malraux, *Antimémoires* (1967), in *Œuvres complètes* (Paris: Gallimard, 1996), 3: 162–192.

† This version of events is confirmed both by note 20 in Gaëtan Picon's *Malraux par lui-même* (Paris: Le Seuil, 1953), 60, and by the prefatory note to the *Antimemoirs*, 7; *Antimémoires*, 3: 13. These are texts that Blanchot would have been able to read at the time of writing *The Instant of My Death*. [For Malraux's prefatory note, see André Malraux, *The Walnut Trees of Altenburg*, trans. A.W. Fielding (Chicago: University of Chicago Press, 1992), v; André Malraux, *Les noyers de l'Altenburg* (1943; 1948), in *Œuvres complètes* (Paris: Gallimard, 1996), 2: 619.]

most ordinary atheism would find amusing. (It is of course my duty here to acknowledge in turn that this scene is the "matrix scene" of my idea—which doesn't belong to me—of a "matrix scene": such is the demonic law.)

I will simply recall the following: the narrator, the one who speaks in the first person—let's call him "Malraux," in scare quotes, for contrary to what happens in the opening of the book, which acts as a counterpart to the epilogue and in which Malraux, in an autobiographical mode, recounts his experience as a prisoner in the camp at Chartres in 1940, the final scene is imaginary—the narrator returns to the world with his squad after having spent an agonizing night in a tank trapped in an "antitank ditch," immobilized and cut off under enemy fire, but from which he was able to extract himself. What is then given to him, as in the instant of birth (supposing birth itself were something one could experience), is the originary appearance of the world, that which, in other words, never appears as such. I am just, only barely, reading; here, too, one would need an endless analysis. (Just moments before, the narrator, having quoted Pascal, says: "Perhaps dread is always the more powerful; perhaps the joy granted to the only animal that knows it is not eternal is poisoned from the very beginning. This morning, however, I am all birth.")[32]

> The world might have been as simple as the sky or the sea. And looking at these shapes in front of me, which are only the shapes of an abandoned, condemned village; looking at these barns of Paradise and these clothes-pegs, these dead fires and these wells, these scattered briars, these voracious brambles which in a year's time will have perhaps overrun everything; these animals, these trees, these houses, I feel myself to be in the presence of an inexplicable gift—an apparition. All this might not have been—might not have been as it is? How all these unique shapes harmonize with the earth! There are other worlds, worlds of crystals, of oceanic depths . . . With its trees branching out like veins, the universe is as full and mysterious as a young body. The door of the farmhouse I am now walking past has been left open by the farmers in their flight: I catch a glimpse of a half-ransacked room. Ah, the three Magi did not bring gifts to the Child, they only told him that on the night he was born, doors were banging in the desolate light, doors half-opened onto the life that is being revealed to me, this morning for the first time, as powerful as the darkness and as powerful as death.*

Then, after meeting an old peasant couple who hadn't fled the fighting—out of indifference, weariness, or resignation—and the woman being the

* Malraux, *The Walnut Trees of Altenburg*, 223; Malraux, *Les noyers de l'Altenburg*, 766.

only one to speak to him, the narrator—"Malraux"—continues, and here is the *nekyia*:

> Attuned to the cosmos like a stone . . . Yet she smiles—a slow, lingering, reflective smile: beyond the football pitch with its solitary goalposts, beyond the tank-turrets glistening with dew like the bushes camouflaging them, she seems to be looking at death in the distance, with patience and even—oh, that mysterious flutter, that sharp shadow in the corner of her eyelids—with irony. . . .
>
> Half-opened doors, washing, barns, traces of mankind, biblical dawn in which the centuries jostle one another—how the whole dazzling mystery of the morning deepens into the mystery surfacing on those worn lips! Let the mystery of mankind reappear in an enigmatic smile, and the resurrection of the earth becomes nothing more than a quivering backdrop.
>
> I know now the meaning of ancient myths about the living being snatched from the dead. I scarcely remember what terror is like; what I carry within me is the discovery of a simple, sacred secret.
>
> Thus, perhaps, did God look on the first man.*

If I have summoned this text, it is not to suggest that Malraux confesses what Blanchot conceals: that myth is at work here—as well as citation, that is, precisely, "life in myth," if indeed it is still a matter, in both cases, of what we call "life" (even though Malraux still speaks of the animal that we are or are supposed to be; Blanchot, in any case, carefully avoids doing so). On the contrary, it seemed to me that if Malraux's name was the only one mentioned in *The Instant of My Death* (along with that of Paulhan, admittedly, but who, in this case, more than the secret overseer of the Gallimard publishing house, is perhaps the author of the famous *Letter to the Directors of the Résistance*, which, soon after the Liberation, in the name perhaps of a certain "right to literature," had called on people not to incriminate indiscriminately writers who were deemed, rightly or wrongly, to have collaborated—that is, not to employ the very methods against which they had fought).† On the contrary,

* Malraux, *The Walnut Trees of Altenburg*, 224; Malraux, *Les noyers de l'Altenburg*, 766–767.

† As Richard Rand pointed out to me (and I thank him for it), there is also a whole "subplot" around Paulhan, the trail of which one would need to follow at least as far as Blanchot's "Pré-Texte" to Dionys Mascolo's *À la recherche d'un communisme de pensée*, written in 1993. [Blanchot's text was subsequently reprinted as a separate volume under the title *Pour l'amitié* (Tours: Farrago, 2000) and also recently collected in *La condition critique*, ed. Christophe Bident (Paris: Gallimard, 2010), 467–478; for an English translation of this text, see "For Friendship," in Maurice Blanchot, *Political Writings, 1953–1993*, ed. and trans. Zakir Paul (New York: Fordham University Press, 2010), 134–143.] I prob-

then, it seemed to me that if Malraux's name was the only one mentioned in *The Instant of My Death*, it is because *The Instant of My Death* responds to *The Walnut Trees of Altenburg*, or indeed to any other book by Malraux, on precisely the question of myth. Not in order to say: no more myth, but to say that where Malraux—to whom Blanchot was at any rate opposed from 1958 onward and whose political trajectory is like the photographic negative of his own trajectory (nation versus justice, or birth versus death, the last judgment)—where Malraux affirms the necessity of myth, Blanchot stubbornly limits himself, or rather strives to limit himself, to a most demanding reserve.

It is not that Blanchot did not give in to myth. He has done so at least as much as any other in this century, even going so far as to propose, long after the "dark days," the Orphic *nekyia* as the myth of the origin of literature or of *poïesis* in its essence, for example. But the one we will henceforth despairingly call the "last Blanchot" will have wanted relentlessly to rid himself of this haunting obsession [*hantise*], which is demonic repetition itself—or the eternal repetition of *re-legere*.

This cannot be done. And *The Instant of My Death*, at the culminating point of its vigilance, at the very moment in which it pulls itself together at the edge of the imminent void, does not escape this ruthless law. There is one remaining paragraph, following the reference to Malraux. It reads—and this is truly abyssal: "What does it matter. There remains only the feeling of lightness that is death itself or, to put it more precisely, the instant of my death henceforth always in abeyance [*en instance*]."*

But this is a citation!

It is at any rate the same "feeling of lightness" that is at the heart (without heart) of the (in)experience of death in the two most famous thanatographical scenes in the French autobiographical tradition, which are themselves already not unrelated, because it is hardly imaginable that Rousseau wouldn't have read Montaigne.

We find the first mention of this in book 2, chapter 6 of the *Essays*: "On Practice," which, incidentally, is entirely determined by the classical exemplarity of learning how to die, that is to say, of philosophizing. The victim of a serious horse-riding accident, Montaigne regains consciousness [*revient à lui*], as we (have to) say (as Rousseau himself says). He writes:

---

ably will return to this later, as well as to the other (impressive) *nekyia* recounted in Malraux's *Lazarus*, a text first published in 1974.

* Blanchot, *The Instant of My Death*, 11; Blanchot, *L'instant de ma mort*, 18.

> My condition was truly most agreeable and peaceful: I felt no affliction either for myself or for others; it was a kind of languor and extreme weakness, without any pain. I saw my house without recognizing it. When they got me into bed, I experienced a feeling of infinite gentleness as I rested, for I had been dreadfully pulled about by those poor fellows who had taken the trouble to carry me in their arms over a long and very poor road and who, one after another, had tired themselves out two or three times. I was offered several medicines: I would not take any of them, being convinced that I was fatally wounded in the head. It would have been, quite honestly, a very happy death, for the weakness of my reasoning powers kept me from judging anything, and that of my body from feeling anything. I let myself ooze away so gently, with such gentleness and such ease, that I can hardly think of any action less grievous than that was.
>
> [. . .]
>
> This account of so light and trivial an event is futile enough but for the instruction I drew from it for my own purposes: for, in truth, to accustom oneself to death, I find that all one has to do is to draw nigh to it.*

The second mention is in the second "Promenade" of the *Reveries*. Once again, it involves an accident. Knocked over by a dog as he is descending from Ménilmontant toward Paris, Rousseau loses consciousness and then, in turn, comes to. I quote just these few lines:

> I felt neither the blow, nor the fall, nor anything of what happened thereafter until I came to.
>
> It was almost night when I regained consciousness. I found myself in the arms of three or four young men who told me what had just happened to me.
>
> [. . .]
>
> The state in which I found myself in that instant is too singular not to be described here.
>
> Night was falling. I saw the sky, a few stars, and a little greenery. This first sensation was a moment of delight. It alone gave me some feeling of myself. In that instant I was born into life, and it seemed to me as if I was filling all the things I saw with my light, frail existence. Completely in the present moment, I remembered nothing; I had no distinct notion of myself as an individual, nor the slightest idea of what had just happened to me; I did not know who I was nor where I was; I felt neither pain, nor fear, nor worry. I saw my blood flowing

* Michel de Montaigne, "On Practice," in *Essays*, trans. M. A. Screech (London: Penguin, 2003), book 2, 422–424; Michel de Montaigne, "De l'exercitation" (1580), in *Les essais*, ed. Pierre Villey (Paris: PUF, 1988), book 2, 376–377.

> as I would have watched a stream flowing, without even thinking that this blood belonged in any way to me. I felt throughout my whole being a wonderful calm with which, whenever I recall it, I find nothing to compare in the whole realm of known pleasures.*

A tone and a style, a posture, a halo of references (a "culture"), a state of language, the circumstances, of course,† and even their intentions, differentiate all of these texts from one another. Yet there are fewer differences between them than one might think. An almost analogous rhythm moves across [*scande*] each one of them: perhaps the (obstinate) basso continuo of mythic repetition through which their individual modulations never cease to sustain themselves. And in truth, they all say the same thing: a strange calm, and, although the word doesn't appear in Malraux (probably because of Hugo), this enigmatic *lightness*, which is a deliverance in every sense of the term.

What is at stake, then, provided that one delivers this deliverance from its meta-physical or eschatological overtones (the liberation from this world) and provided one refrains from dreaming, in death, of a hope of *sur*vival—and I'm not forgetting a word of what you've written on that subject, in relation precisely to Blanchot—what is at stake, then, is an innocence like that with which, not at all by accident, we credit *in-fantia* ("as innocent as a new-born child"), that happy state before language, or, I will say, given the occasion: before *mythos*. The final *nekyia* that we are invited to read here—but I know full well that it is illegible without recalling "A Primal Scene" ("suppose, suppose this: the child [. . .]");[33] I'll return to this elsewhere, as I must—states nothing other than this hope for in-nocence (an altogether different hope from that of survival) and proposes, perhaps, at the edge of silence, nothing other than the discreet effacement of myth—that is to say, of evil. A final citation no longer to be cited.

People can say what they like about Blanchot's political and intellectual fate and even about his literary "absolutism." "What does it matter." Blanchot will have been one of the few in this century, and even in this era that opened up between Terror ("Literature and the Right to Death") and the Cult of the

* Jean-Jacques Rousseau, *Reveries of the Solitary Walker*, trans. Russell Goulbourne (Oxford: Oxford University Press, 2011), 14; Jean-Jacques Rousseau, *Les rêveries du promeneur solitaire* (1782), in *Œuvres complètes* (Paris: Gallimard, 1959), 1:1005.

† On the face of it an accident (a "fall") cannot be compared to an execution or even to a "mock" or "thwarted" execution (though that remains to be seen). But the same is true of illness; yet there is *Lazarus*. The (in)experience of death in fact owes little to circumstances; I'll try to show this in relation to "A Primal Scene."

Supreme Being—let's call it the epoch of the religion of the political, which in fact coincides with the romantic invention of literature—to understand and to say, at his own expense and through a difficulty that went so far as to disqualify and preclude any "self-criticism," that it is remythologization alone that bears the responsibility for evil.

One may—one *must*—still relentlessly ponder the following now-famous proposition:

> But how many saw that Hitler's despotism was not a tyranny of a sort that had already existed, but that if he was so relentless in his persecution of Judaism and of the Jews, it was because the latter incarnated, in the highest degree, not only the refusal of all forms of servitude—they, the slaves who came out of Egypt—but the rejection of myths, the forswearing of idols, and the recognition of an ethical order manifesting itself in respect for the Law. In the Jew, in the "myth of the Jew," what Hitler wanted to annihilate was, precisely, mankind freed from myths.*

I will come back to—and ponder—this proposition, since, as I keep saying, I have not done with my demon. But when I do, shortly, I will do so as I have done ever since the day when, ten years ago, on the only academic occasion at which I was summoned to appear before you,[34] you asked me, responding, softly, anxiously, to my peremptory (though well-intentioned) affirmation that there was nothing sacrificial about the Extermination (the "Disaster"): "Are you so sure of that?"

If I came here today, it was also to tell you that I did indeed hear you then.

* Maurice Blanchot, "Intellectuals Under Scrutiny," in *The Blanchot Reader*, ed. and trans. Michael Holland (Oxford: Blackwell, 1995), 221; Maurice Blanchot, *Les intellectuels en question* (1984; Tours: Farrago, 2000), 47–48.

The Contestation of Death

The Instant of My Death may well be Maurice Blanchot's testamentary book.

This very short narrative [*récit*], if indeed it is a "narrative," in which, as is known, Maurice Blanchot recounts how on July 20, 1944, he experienced "the happiness of nearly being shot dead" (those were his words, reported by Jacques Derrida),* was considered to be such by a number of us when it was published six years ago.

"Testamentary book" can be understood in various ways; the word, the concept of testament (attestation, testimony, etc.), are among the most difficult to think rigorously, and I'm aware of the numerous analyses that were recently devoted to them, even though in some cases, their cunning virtuosity seems to me to be, precisely, *contestable*. (I will return at some point to what unites and divides "attest," "contest," "protest," "detest," "test," among other terms.)[1] I take "testamentary book" to mean here, in the simplest way possible, "last book": the last book by Maurice Blanchot, the last words uttered or written for publication—under the authority, if one may venture such a term, of the three instances that will have governed (or disoriented), organized (or unworked [*désœuvré*]), what we must resign ourselves to calling his work, however impossible it might be to delimit its configuration: Politics (or History), the Experience of death, and Literature. But at the same time, "last book" also means just that: *the last book*, the last words spoken by the "last to speak," the final words—the end of literature.

"End," in turn, is yet another word that can be understood in more than one sense: conclusion [*achèvement*] (termination, cessation), completion [*accomplissement*] (finishing), and aim [*but visé*] (according to what is called the finality principle). For my part, I would happily emphasize a further mean-

* Jacques Derrida, *Demeure: Fiction and Testimony*, trans. Elizabeth Rottenberg (Stanford, Calif.: Stanford University Press, 1998), 52; Jacques Derrida, *Demeure: Maurice Blanchot* (Paris: Galilée, 1998), 64.

ing, derived from the Aristotelian interpretation of the *telos* but entirely reworked by modern thought from Rousseau and Kant onward: where the end is thought as the origin itself. Which doesn't mean "beginning," still less "cause," although Aristotle did conceive of the *telos* within the framework of his theory of causality or, more accurately, of his onto-etiology. Nor does it mean "essence," a word that Maurice Blanchot nonetheless used a great deal in connection with literature in such phrases as: the essence of literature is to move toward its own essence, which is its disappearance. It means, rather, *condition* of possibility, and I emphasize the transcendental concept of "condition," which others would translate as "negativity" or "mediation" (Hegel or Hölderlin, for example), to indicate accurately the register in which the logic of origin operates, which, despite the speculative *doxa*, is indeed the register of finitude.

In this way, and provided of course that one accepts these premises, it should be clear that if *The Instant of My Death* is the "last book" (by Maurice Blanchot), it signifies the end of Literature only insofar as its sole end is to indicate its origin. The death of Literature, then, would be its birth. And so at stake would be less its essence than its very existence—or, to put it even more bluntly, its right to existence.

(I open here a brief parenthesis, as an internal exclusion: at stake, then, is an impossible place, as is that of existence *itself.* And consequently the place, also, that *must be* occupied or *inhabited*, as well as the place where, probably, *there are*, together, the three instances I mentioned just now: Politics, the Experience of death, and Literature.

In addition to his questionable political illusions (and, as their counterpart, his "narcissistic" indulgence),* Blanchot has been much accused, of late, of having been the victim of a historicist and teleological conception of literature, derived no doubt from Mallarmé—but has Blanchot ever concealed his debt, and the immense difficulty therein?—and, beyond Mallarmé, at times from Jena romanticism, at others from Hegel, that is to say, from Kojève-Bataille just as well, when it wasn't from Heidegger. Some of the undoubtedly and deliberately blunt propositions I have just formulated appear to "dialectize" and could lead one to think that I thereby confirm—and approve of—that "filiation," so to speak. This would call for careful examination. But not *here*; this is not the "place" for it.

What I would like to put forward, on the other hand, and this is therefore

* I will return elsewhere to this motif, notably in relation to the fragment "(A Primal Scene?)" in *The Writing of the Disaster.* [See "Ending and Unending Agony," in the present volume.]

really my first hypothesis, is that there is no literature—or, let's face it, there is no literary work—that does not wish to be *definitive*. What literature wants or seeks, since some such thing exists, if it exists, is its end: that is to say, the secret of its origin, the condition (rule, law, prohibition) that it must undergo to be possible. What literature wants or seeks—we all ought to know this and take it into account—is the impossible.

I now close the parenthesis.)

And I thus advance my second hypothesis.

The "lesson" of *The Instant of My Death*, its testamentary legacy, if you will, is to affirm that to write—that is, to write "in its strongest sense [*au sens majeur*]," as Roger Laporte put it, whose unique work, *Une vie*, concludes, comes to completion, and ends with a volume entitled, precisely, *Moriendo*—is not to recount how one lives or, what amounts to the same thing, how others live, whatever modality of time one might choose. Rather, writing is to say how one has died. And that is the very practice of thought, which is not to be surprised or to wonder at the fact that "I am" but to endure the fact that "I have no longer been," that perhaps "I am already no more" or that "I have never been," and to be overwhelmed, devastated by it—which, strictly speaking, defines existence; I hope to say a few words about this later.

The experience of death—that pure impossibility—would thus be the condition, end, and origin, if not the categorical imperative (the unconditioned "one must [*il faut*]"), of literature and, equally, of thought.

I set aside, for now, the reference I have just made to thought and, by the same token, to ethics—the two are indeed indissociable.

I will limit myself—or try to limit myself—to literature alone.

From the standpoint of *The Instant of My Death*, of the limit or end that this book represents today—that is to say, provisionally (the said "end of Literature" is infinite; it is, in theory, unending)—three things at least seem to me worth noting:

1. The recurrence of analogous scenes, not only, as one might expect, in Blanchot's work (for example, *Death Sentence*, *The Madness of the Day*, and *The Writing of the Disaster*), or even only in that of Bataille, which is very close to it, particularly in the texts written during the war (*Inner Experience*, "The Practice of Joy Before Death"), but also in some of the monuments of the literature contemporaneous with Blanchot or that Blanchot deemed to be contemporaneous with his own.

I will take but a few examples, briefly, and from French literature alone.

There is the obvious case of the same scene, or very nearly the same, in 1944, recounted by Malraux, albeit in a "scatty [*farfelu*]" mode (as he would have said), in the *Antimemoirs* (a significant title, as Maurice Blanchot knew very well, having written about it). That it may have been suggested by a well-known letter by Dostoyevsky, "mythomania" playing its part too, matters fairly little, nor does it matter that it is treated "with cheek [*à la gouaille*]": *Lazarus* is also there, close at hand, with its far greater gravity, and tells the same "experience without experience" or "unexperienced experience" (these are Blanchot's expressions) of death. There is, furthermore, the story that Artaud tells of his own death while undergoing electroshock treatment, at Rodez—or, what amounts to the same thing, on Golgotha two thousands years ago—in the famous "Vieux-Colombier Lecture" (I spoke of this elsewhere).[2] That this may have been suggested by the Nietzsche of *Ecce Homo*, among others ("as my father I am dead already, and as my mother I am still alive and growing old"),[3] hardly matters either, despite the enigma of identification: with Christ, with Dionysus, with both of them at once. Among these "cases," and I could cite others, there is, in our literary tradition, Mallarmé, as is well known—and Hegel, yes, undeniably: I'm thinking of the "I am completely and utterly dead" in the letter to Cazalis[4] or his "Destruction was my Beatrice,"[5] and so many poems. And as a result, one should also add Baudelaire's hell or Rimbaud's *Season*, not to lay too much emphasis on Chateaubriand's *Memoirs from Beyond the Grave*, the title of which speaks for itself, to say the least.

It has been said recently that this paradox of the impossible possibility (of the experience) of death owes much to Poe—given Baudelaire and Mallarmé. An age or century of Poe was even suggested, overdetermined by English romanticism and the English fantastic. (But why not German romanticism and the German fantastic? Where does Poe come from, if not, via Coleridge, from Schelling? And isn't Kafka's "The Hunter Gracchus" one of Blanchot's major references outside the Jena circle?) Maurice Blanchot would thus still be indebted to the "century of Poe" and as such would be "dated." And Poe, in this instance, would be reduced to the well-known—and evidently impossible—statement uttered by Monsieur de Valdemar: "You see full well that I am dead!"[6]

Let's assume this nevertheless—for a moment. After all, in our Letters, as we say, no one is ignorant of the role played by Poe, of his importance; so much so that in many respects, he can be considered as a "French author." And of course, his place in *Weltliteratur* cannot be underestimated.

But just as I drew attention to the "Malraux case"—and Malraux is *named* in *The Instant of My Death*—in the same way, two years ago, during a discussion at Cerisy-la-Salle with Jacques Derrida regarding precisely that text, I thought it necessary to mention, in light of our so-called autobiographical tradition and thus of our supposedly nonfictional literature, two precedents of the "scene" of the unexperienced experience of death, both of them preceding the romantic age (and the appearance of the *concept* of Literature): the story Montaigne tells of his fall from a horse, in chapter 6 of book 2 of the *Essays*: "On Practice," and the second "Promenade" in Rousseau's *Reveries*, which may rightly be considered as a citation of Montaigne, less because of the accident mentioned (a violent fall, in both cases) as on another account, less often mentioned, which is that Rousseau finds in Montaigne the precise formulation of the *paradox* enabling him to grasp his "feeling of existence."[7]

I quote, for the record:

> But practice is no help in the greatest task we have to perform: dying.
>
> [...]
>
> Yet it seems to me that we have some means of accustoming ourselves to it [death] and to some extent trying it. We can *experience* it [my emphasis], if not wholly or completely then at least in such a way that it is not useless and that makes us more strong and steadfast. If we cannot join battle with it, we can approach it, we can reconnoiter it; and if we cannot reach its stronghold, we can at least glimpse and explore approaches to it.*

It is true that Montaigne's words are inscribed—in fact, deliberately so—in a vast tradition of ancient wisdom and meditations on death: the famous chapter 20 of book 1 alone, so often misunderstood: "To Philosophize Is to Learn How to Die" already made this clear. One could draw nothing but a somewhat pedantic, assiduous accumulation of *topoi* from remarks of this sort. Still, by way of an anecdote borrowed from Seneca, Montaigne doesn't refrain from radicalizing the paradox of the "*experience*" of death, since such is indeed the word he uses, speaking of "philosophizing not merely until death but into death itself,"[8] and especially since he is describing a real experience, where the paradox of possible-impossible death is not simply resolved in the mode of the "as if" or of the "semblance of" (and still less of the "quasi" or of the "nearly"), or even in the mode of an approach (Montaigne speaks of "drawing nigh to" death),[9] but where, on the contrary, that paradox maintains itself and hardens or congeals in the sudden, stupefying manifestation of the "feeling of existence" (of the *fact* of being), which, in the three texts in

* Michel de Montaigne, "On Practice," in *Essays*, trans. M.A. Screech (London: Penguin, 2003), book 2, 416–417; Michel de Montaigne, "De l'exercitation," in *Les essais*, ed. Pierre Villey (Paris: PUF, 1988), book 2, 371–372.

question, is identified each time with a "feeling of lightness," of detachment, of inexplicable elation. In short, in the same way as it is summarized in the last sentence of Blanchot's short "narrative": "There remains only the feeling of lightness that is death itself or, to put it more precisely, the instant of my death henceforth always in abeyance."*

Perhaps this is quite simply the feeling of *immortality*, which is at the origin of what we call ethics. And I'm not thinking only of Spinoza, of this or that proposition in his *Ethics* claiming that we feel or experience ourselves to be immortal. I'm also thinking of the *Phaedo*, of which I'll speak again later and which was so scandalously ill-treated by antiquity's scholastic tradition—and by everything that followed it.

2. One could argue, and I, for my part, would gladly argue, that literature as we still understand it (in its "modern" sense) is not born—if it was indeed born once, somewhere—with the novel, which derives from the epic form, but with *auto-biography*.

But one sees immediately the countless questions that arise here.

Where, for example, can this autobiography be said to begin, where can one situate its end as it presents itself for the first time as origin? With the early modern period, between Dante and Montaigne? With Christianity and the experience of confession (Saint Augustine)? Or earlier, with Plato himself, the Plato of "Epistle 7," for example? Or with the Platonic and Neoplatonic tradition?

Does this genre—but is it a genre, as classical genre theory would understand it?—when it was established (because such a thing surely must have taken place), imply a transformation of the *autos*, of the *ego*, of the "I" or of the Self, in short, of what in effect we call, since the dawn of modernity, the subject? Does it have a bearing upon the mode of enunciation? And if a profound transformation of the *autos*, etc., must be supposed, does that necessarily mean that this "genre" is enclosed within what Heidegger, with and against Hegel, marked out as a "metaphysics of subjectity,"[10] stretching from Descartes to Nietzsche and beyond? Or must one think instead that for a book such as the *Discourse on Method* to come to light or be possible, a "genre" of autobiography must have already existed?

And what understanding of the said "experience" is at stake behind this "subject"? Is it "lived experience," *Erlebnis*, as Heidegger would have doubtless hastened to say? Yet what relation would this "lived experience" hold

* Maurice Blanchot, *The Instant of My Death*, trans. Elizabeth Rottenberg (Stanford, Calif.: Stanford University Press, 1998), 11; Maurice Blanchot, *L'instant de ma mort* (1994; Paris: Gallimard, 1998), 18.

with the *bios*, which, hardly by accident, makes its way, in Greek, into the concept of *bio-graphy*, as it was the case (previously?) in phrases or titles à la Plutarch: *Parallel Lives*, etc.? Or is it ex-perience, in the strict sense: the journey through (*ex-*) a peril (*periri*); in German: *Er-fahrung* (*fahren*, *Gefahr*, etc.)?[11] And what relation would experience understood in this way maintain, in Latin, with trial [*épreuve*], in the various senses of the word: affective, judiciary, narrative, religious, scientific, etc.? Up to which point does experience (or trial), in the language of mysticism or philosophy, imply, as Bataille would say, "putting *life* itself at risk"?

I obviously cannot answer all of these questions, the number of which I'm in fact already restricting here.

What I would simply like to point out, on the basis of the few examples I have mentioned, is that if autobiography in general, in its end as in its origin, implies an *experience* in the strict sense, and if this experience is consistently identified with a journey through (or a trial of) death, as infinitely paradoxical or impossible as that might be, then one is at the very least bound to change its "generic" index and to speak—*at the very least*—of *autothanatography*. Such a proposition or formulation is neither new nor original. It was developed by several of us more than twenty years ago, namely, around the work of Roger Laporte. But I think it is possible still to lay claim to it, *at least* within certain limits.

It is plausible that within the concept of *ex-perience* or within the phrase "journey through death [*traversée de la mort*]" there remain concealed or veiled the vestiges of very ancient initiatory and mythico-epic schemata. I have had occasion, on the subject of Artaud (but Nietzsche, for example, would lead one to think along the same lines just as much), to recall the ancient *nekyia*: the descent to Hell and the presentation of the dead, which makes up the (exact) center of the *Odyssey*, of the *Aeneid*, perhaps even of the *Pharsalia*, and which, as can be seen, repeats itself ceaselessly, from Dante to Poe and Rimbaud, right up to the present. That is to say, *at least* right up to Maurice Blanchot, and I'm also thinking, in this instance, of the use he made of the myth of Orpheus to indicate precisely the end of Literature as its origin. The remanence of myths, or their somber, stormy redeployment, is perhaps that to which one must not consent or what one should *contest*. Yet one cannot but notice [*constater*] it here.

3. A last remark, then: I mentioned very briefly, just moments ago, the possibility of a transformation in the mode of enunciation at the end of "autobiography," as well as at its origin. I was thinking, first, as goes without saying, of the Platonic tripartition of the modes of enunciation: diegetic,

mimetic, and mixed,[12] which, via a few misunderstandings, is at the source of the tripartition of genres in classical theory: lyric, dramatic, and epic. The diegetic mode being the mode reputed to be proper to the *autos* or to the *ego* (to the "I"): "I, here, in person, speak and say that . . . ," it was eventually inferred from this that lyricism is a "subjective genre," which, incidentally, almost proved fatal to it. Now, neither in Plato's dithyramb nor in classical or modern lyricism, nor even in the oratorical genre, is there a place for the said "subject" of autobiography. Unless one considers Montaigne to be a lyric poet, and such things are indeed tried, in school textbooks, on Rousseau. . . . The subject of autobiography, if there is one, has to be of an entirely different consistency. And if this "genre" is to be called, resolutely, *autothanatography*, then it is no longer a question, de jure, of a *subject* (*subjectum*, or even *substantia*). And if it is indeed an "I" that speaks there, which remains to be shown, it probably no longer has the slightest *con-sistency*, and nothing guarantees that it remains, or even quite simply is, itself or the same: *autos, ho autos*. What kind of "subject" could articulate: "I am dead"?

That is why, moreover, I thought the following: to my knowledge, there are only two overtly "autobiographical" texts by Maurice Blanchot: *The Instant of My Death* and that short page, detached like a fragment in *The Writing of the Disaster*, entitled "(A Primal Scene?)," for which, moreover, there is a first version with a much less suspensive or more definitive title: "A Primal Scene."* (Other seemingly "autobiographical" texts, such as *Vicious Circles*, *Foucault as I Imagine Him*, *The Unavowable Community*, perhaps even the (unpublished) "Memorandum,"[13] are rather of the order, I won't say of testimony (true or false, it matters little), but of *attestation*: an *other*, de facto (Dionys Mascolo, for example) or de jure (the anonymous crowd of the revolutionaries, or, as euphemism has it, of the "protesters [*contestataires*]" of May '68), de facto *and* de jure (those just mentioned, and Bataille, who died in 1962, but Levinas too, et al.), could put this attestation to the *proof* [*à l'épreuve*], which is *always* possible: to prove it or invalidate it, whatever views are held on the matter by all those (and they are legion) who pervert Celan's words: "No one bears witness for the witness."[14] As soon as there is testimony, or *attestation*, an other, whoever that may be, is *always* implicated, that is, *contested* (*cum-testari*) in the strict sense. Would that this had not to be recalled, even so elliptically.)

The Instant of My Death and "(A Primal Scene?)," then. A childhood

* Published in *Première Livraison* 4 (February–March 1976), ed. Mathieu Bénézet and Philippe Lacoue-Labarthe. [See "Ending and Unending Agony," in the present volume.]

scene and the scene of death—supposing they are indeed "scenes." Maurice Blanchot will have thus applied [*opéré*], more effectively than Nicholas of Cusa, the (almost) pure reduction of "autobiography."

Now, what is remarkable and difficult in these two texts is that Maurice Blanchot speaks of himself—or of "him"—in the third person, even though the enunciative "I," or the "I" thus perceived, intervenes explicitly in *The Instant of My Death* (for example: "In his place [in the place of "the man still young," who is the "character" of the "narrative"], I will not try to analyze this feeling of lightness";[15] the verb, left as it was in the manuscript, is in the future tense, leaving the enigma entirely unresolved) and indirectly, by means of an address, in "(A Primal Scene?)": "You who live later, close to a heart that beats no more, suppose, suppose this: the child. . . ."[16] This strange dissociation of the "subject" in question is not that implied by the general phenomenon of enunciation (it is at least *re-marked* upon), nor is it of the same order as that of classical narrative enunciation, and we know, besides, that Blanchot explicitly and even solemnly repudiated or dismissed narrative as such, notably in the final sentence of *The Madness of the Day*. Yet one cannot but wonder, were it only because of the address itself, in its form and its "impossible" meaning: "You who live later . . . ," whether Maurice Blanchot doesn't reveal, in a single stroke, the mode of all supposedly "autobiographical" enunciation, which is decidedly *autothanatographical*, since the "subject" evidently must somehow be *dead already* in order for it to begin to say itself and write itself *as an other*: so that it may accept to summon "itself" or contest "itself," thereby summoning or contesting death (or the dead one) in himself, producing together the witnesses of both parties.

In which case, autothanatography is in truth always, to venture a somewhat simple term, *allobiography*.[17]

It is at any rate no accident if both these texts involve, each time, an ecstasy at the heart of the "narrative." In *The Unavowable Community*, Blanchot says of ecstasy (with Bataille in mind): "Its decisive feature is that he who experiences it is no longer there when he experiences it, is therefore no longer there to experience it."* Yet it takes place nevertheless: *there is* ecstasy. The structure here is rigorously the same as that of the "experience without experience" or "unexperienced experience" of death: *I is an other* in a far more radical sense, probably, than that which Rimbaud gave the expression he coined (even though there is the *Season*, and Rimbaud "operated on himself

* Maurice Blanchot, *The Unavowable Community*, trans. Pierre Joris (Barrytown, N.Y.: Station Hill, 1988), 19; Maurice Blanchot, *La communauté inavouable* (Paris: Minuit, 1983), 37.

while wide awake, removing poetry,"[18] as Mallarmé put it). That is why death is *immemorial*, just like birth, and has always already deposed the subject. *The Writing of the Disaster* reads as follows: "Dying means: *you* [my emphasis] are dead already, in an immemorial past, of a death which was not yours. . . . This uncertain death, always anterior, an *attestation* [my emphasis again] of a past without present, is never individual."*

Autothanatography (allobiography)—and this is true of Montaigne, of Rousseau, of so many others—is the mode, I dare not say genre or form, of the *desistance* [désistance] of the subject, if I may use here a word generously bestowed upon me by Jacques Derrida.[19] The subject disappears therein, collapses, withdraws, and fades away; it has in truth already disappeared, retired from itself, taciturn (*infans*), absent (as is said of someone who is not paying attention), lost, yet it remains or returns to say, in another voice (exactly the same), what happened without it (with it and within it), an impossible attestation, a testimony for which there is no witness but that it persists in producing, because "it" was (not) there and because "it" was (not) it(self). The relentlessness with which Blanchot assigned the "birth" of Literature to the passage from the first to the third person, from the "I" to the "he," if not to the impersonal "it," is well known. That is perhaps what, after all, is essentially being *challenged* in the "autobiographical" *process* or *trial* [procès]; with or without defense, it matters not, just as the sincerity or accuracy of the testimony—its veracity—is irrelevant. The *litigation* and the *contestation* alone are what counts: as in the old word "litiscontester" (*litem contestari*), which meant "to bring proceedings."

It is at any rate this device [*dispositif*] that brings me now to propose here a final hypothesis, which is no doubt more "contentious [*litigieuse*]" than those preceding but which I feel I must submit to judgment.

Coming back to Montaigne, considered in this particular case to be the initiator of the "genre"—obviously a shortcut, and a drastic one—two aspects, it seems to me, require emphasis.

The first has long since been emphasized—I hardly need to make it stand out here: it is the predominance, in all meditations on death, of the Socratic *exemplum* and the constant reference to Plato's *Phaedo*. Undoubtedly, beneath the care for wisdom and for the *care* itself for death (for the *melete tou thanatou*,[20] the cultivation of death or the process of "accustoming ourselves

* Maurice Blanchot, *The Writing of the Disaster*, trans. Ann Smock (Lincoln: University of Nebraska Press, 1995), 65–66; Maurice Blanchot, *L'écriture du désastre* (Paris: Gallimard, 1980), 108–109.

to [it]"), the whole of ancient ethics, including the Romans' *cura*, is being summoned, from the preaching of the Stoics to the arguments of Epicurus and Lucretius. But Socrates remains the only example of a philosopher who philosophizes dying and who dies from practicing philosophy—an inaugural figure, then, deciding that death is the condition of thought itself. There is no need to insist: this is the case for the whole philosophical tradition, including Nietzsche and Heidegger.

The second aspect is less often noted. It is nonetheless clear. For, the episode of the fall from the horse recounted in the chapter "On Practice" is actually about an ambush and a military and political incident. Montaigne doesn't say so expressly. But he situates the scene "during our third disturbances or the second,"[21] and the expression indeed designates the wars of religion (which Montaigne calls in fact "civil wars," writing, for example, that he "sits in the midst of all the disturbances of France's civil wars");[22] he refers, as explicitly as possible, to the Protestants ("our neighbors");[23] he speaks of "harquebusades,"[24] which were numerous during the incident and which in all likelihood caused his horse to bolt. He was no doubt not a target himself: it was not an attempt on his life—rather, a kind of unforeseen chance "skirmish" at most, as happens in "guerrilla warfare," whereas Montaigne thought he was "entirely safe and so near [his] dwelling"[25] (the scene takes place in the vicinity of his castle, at the edge of the Périgord). But one mustn't forget the significance of Montaigne's political role during that whole period, not only in Bordeaux but also at court and, above all, in connection with Henry of Navarre, whose conversion to Catholicism he is said—it is indeed plausible—to have encouraged in order to guarantee the succession of the French throne and restore "civil" order. Montaigne could thus be, with Bodin, one of the very first political thinkers, at least in France, to envision the reality of the nation-state as it was being formed, which is less "voluntary servitude" as such—inherited all the same by La Boétie from Nicholas of Cusa*—than subjection or subjugation, via religion, to politics or to the political as a whole, which itself slowly becomes "life" in its entirety.

I would not insist on the political aura that, in Montaigne, surrounds his "experience" of death if it were not found in almost all the "narratives" I have mentioned in connection with *The Instant of My Death*: in that of Malraux, for example, it is rather obvious, but also in that of Artaud, who was subjected, for want of being able to flee, to the repression directed against the "avant-gardes" of "degenerate art" and to the unspeakable psychiatric policy

* I owe this observation to Étienne Balibar, for which I thank him.

of the Vichy regime, and if it were not also found, although less markedly or clearly so, in Blanchot's own "narrative" and in that of Rousseau.

As with Montaigne's, and as with Malraux's, Blanchot's "narrative" appears to belong to the genre—it is surely a genre—of the "war narrative." One need only reread the opening to be quickly convinced of this. Now, while the episode is indeed situated at a given moment of the war—that of the counteroffensive attempted by the German Army and in particular by the "Das Reich" SS division against the Allied forces following the Normandy landings in June 1944—there is no suggestion that Blanchot was involved as a combatant (he is at most an accomplice of or a sympathizer with the young peasants of the area, a hamlet in the Haute-Saône where Blanchot's family had its home, who are fighting in the maquis). On the other hand, every effort is made to suggest that there is in fact a *civil war* (and a social war) brewing beneath the ongoing military operations, however much they were global in scope and particularly spectacular: the presence of the SS officer who "shamefully"[26] speaks French, the Russian soldiers of the Vlasov army, the final allusion to the recovery, if not the purging, of the *Nouvelle Revue française* and the Gallimard publishing house implicated in the Collaboration (what goes for the encounter with Malraux and Paulhan goes just as much for Drieu la Rochelle's suicide). Several clues of this kind lead one to think that the episode is part of the long ideological and political struggle that has divided the French intelligentsia since the 1930s, if not the 1920s, a struggle in which, as everyone knows full well, Blanchot took part as a recognized representative of and mouthpiece for the nationalist (Maurrassian) far Right, if not of and for a "French-style fascism" (albeit anti-Nazi or anti-Hitlerian), up to 1938 (Munich), if not to 1942–1943 (when he meet Bataille).[27] That is why, moreover, *The Instant of My Death* can also be read as the "narrative" of a deliverance and a redemption—or a defense. In it, death is *contested*, the "almost dead" in Blanchot, that is, the "always already dead" in him (the other that "he" is), is summoned as the witness of a conversion or of a radical break [*rupture*]. And suddenly, as if by miracle, he is freed from death and from the *mortiferous*—in the name of another politics, without injustice or anything unjustifiable, whose sole intention will be to loosen the grip of the political and whose furtive irruption will be recognized by Blanchot in May 1968. In other words, in the name of a *survival* that is perhaps nothing other—at any rate nothing more—than existence. (And it mustn't be forgotten that this text was written in July 1994, that is, at a time in our recent history in which certain intellectuals, (turned) "humanists" at little cost, and dissatisfied, it would appear, with the intellectual purges, were making repeated and more or less vengeful insinuations about Blanchot's "fascist," "anti-Semite" (etc.)

past, evidently relieved to be able to relativize or diminish Blanchot's difficulty, exigency, and intransigence.)

But that is the case again, all things being equal, in Rousseau's "Second Promenade," Rousseau being perhaps the first in this tradition to dramatize the theme of injustice, wrong, and persecution. I needn't recall how, once the incident is recounted (inasmuch as it is possible to make a "narrative" of one's own absence to oneself), Rousseau's text seems to get lost or incomprehensibly stuck in what is said to be a long "paranoiac" digression (the episode takes place in the very year in which Rousseau attempted in vain to place the manuscript of the *Dialogues* (*Rousseau* Judge [my emphasis] *of Jean-Jacques*) on the high altar of Notre-Dame in Paris and distributed his lampoon *To All Frenchmen Who Still Love* Justice [my emphasis again] *and Truth* in the street): the following day, all of Paris knew about it; his enemies rejoiced; he was attacked (by the police, by Madame d'Ormoy); a forged edition of writings attributed to him was being prepared; a provincial newspaper announced his death, etc. One can laugh or feel sympathy. But that is to be blind: Rousseau's persecution was very real; at least since the publication of *Emile* and *The Social Contract*, books that were burned and condemned, Rousseau had been censured, pursued, scorned, banned, betrayed by the very people he might have thought to be his friends, humiliated, travestied, and ridiculed, compelled to wander restlessly. This was in 1776–1777: intellectual and religious (politico-religious) civil war was raging, a very real war, however much it might have been hidden behind indifference. An *event* was brewing, and it was Rousseau's voice that bore the signs of it.

If this review is even remotely justified—and once again, for each of the names I have come to mention in passing, I could offer an analysis of the same sort—then a very simple truth comes to the fore: the autothanatographical (allobiographical) situation is nothing other than the Socratic situation: an endemic state of civil war, of a truly *political* war (that is, the *stasis* so dreaded by the Greeks); a thinker, who is also a player on the political stage, and in many ways a revolutionary one, even though Plato makes him out to be the most illustrious of reactionaries; an accumulation of hatreds, calumny, accusations of all sorts, mostly made on a religious basis (impiety, the revelation of the "mysteries" . . .); a public trial and condemnation, and death—a death accepted, if not invoked, as the gesture of thought itself: of philosophizing.

I don't bring up Socrates here again, particularly the Socrates of the *Phaedo*, to infer that all so-called autobiographical projects necessarily obey the Socratic *exemplum* and its citation. Nor do I bring him up, obviously, even if I alluded to the feeling of "immortality," to bring into play the metaphysical treatment [*opération*] that Plato—who was not present when it occurred—devised around Socrates's death. I bring him up, rather, because I believe—and Blanchot reminds us of this (I will come to it shortly)—that what is at stake in that death pertains to Literature itself.

Nietzsche once said, in a note more or less contemporaneous with *The Birth of Tragedy*, that Plato had essentially "invented the novel of antiquity."[28] The observation is seductive but doesn't seem quite right to me. If he invented anything, it would rather be what we still call all too hastily "autobiography": an absent enunciator, marked as such and referring to himself ("That day," it is written, "Plato was not present");[29] another, referred to and named (he, Socrates) but who utters the very words attributed to him by the one then absent, as if he were in no way speaking "in person" but in a kind of absence to himself, and who thinks, as he dies, his own (?) thoughts, in a state of detachment, of calm, almost the lightness of consent to death; a feeling of immortality, which Plato hastens to translate and to fix in the language of proof (of *logos*) but which Plato him "self" could not not understand as a "You are dead already"—or else, why would he have written on behalf (and at the incitement?) of he who didn't write and perhaps, by "himself," wouldn't have left any trace of his existence? Or a few platitudes reported by Xenophon and the doxographers? And I say nothing of the constant recalling of the injustice—and the unjustifiability—of a condemnation that is never anything other than the exact consequence of political injustice in general. And all injustice is political.

Maurice Blanchot rarely quoted or recalled Socrates. The name comes up only twice in *The Writing of the Disaster*.[30] The second occurrence is on the page that immediately precedes the long fragment: "Dying means: you are dead already. . . ." Although I certainly did not comment on these lines here, they have been constantly in my sight:

> ♦ Granted, Socrates does not write; but, beneath the voice, it is nevertheless through writing that he gives himself to others as both the perpetual subject and perpetually destined to die. He does not speak; he questions. Questioning, he interrupts and interrupts himself ceaselessly, giving form ironically to the fragmentary and, through death, dooms speech to the haunting [*hantise*] of writing and the latter to testamentary writing alone (with no signature, however).*

* Blanchot, *The Writing of the Disaster*, 65; Blanchot, *L'écriture du désastre*, 107.

At the beginning, I placed *The Instant of My Death* under the authority of three instances that govern the work of Maurice Blanchot right up to its last pages: Politics, the Experience of death, and Literature (I can now say: Writing), brought together as the practice of thought itself. Now we find them again, at the end, and Blanchot himself consents to this, in Plato's *Phaedo*, that is, in one of the inaugural texts of Western philosophy, which, since it offers itself as the impossible autobiography of Socrates ("he who did not write"), is nothing other, after all, than the founding text of *contestation*—the contestation of death (as well as that of political *protestation*). I do not know whether the *Phaedo* is the *birth*place of literature, in other words, of autothanatography (of allobiography). What I glimpse is that it marks an *origin*, and therefore an *end*, and that no literature, in its unending end, can claim to be quits with, or acquitted of, that end as origin.

Note

I said in passing that "I will return at some point to what unites and divides 'attest,' 'contest,' 'protest,' 'detest,' 'test,' among other terms." From the viewpoint of philology alone, this would require a whole field of expertise, which of course I do not have and which would go beyond the mere observation of an *etymon* common to all these words. Given that I deliberately borrowed the term "contestation" from Bataille's vocabulary (a term that, at least since *Inner Experience*, was one of his watchwords), I will limit myself to indicating the following, which is rather elementary: if "to test" (*testari*) is "to call to witness," as well as "to write a last will and testament," it goes almost without saying that all "autobiographical" literature is "testamentary," if not "testimonial." An infinite number of conclusions can be drawn from this; after so many others, I will not venture to draw conclusions myself. But testimony or attestation always presupposes a conflict between arguments "for" and "against," between being in favor of and being hostile to—in other words, as any juridical vocabulary has it, litigation. Hence my reference, which I thought necessary, to the trial and death of Socrates, to his "political" contestation or detestation of a disgraceful religiosity and of injustice, to the protestation of his innocence, as well as to the strange "testimony" of Plato (the "absent" one). It matters little that what we call, since Kant, Nietzsche, or Heidegger, "metaphysics" has its origins in the *Phaedo*, and it matters little, moreover, that Platonic politics, if not already Socratic politics, were markedly "reactionary": they could just as well be "revolutionary" (a formidable word), as we know all too well, unfortunately—and we remain "revolted" by it.

The important thing, in *this* case, is that the *Phaedo* may be considered as the origin, and therefore the condition, of what we call "literature."

I am not saying this to "exonerate" Blanchot, who was the first to know and regret it. In April 1987, in a long letter addressed to Roger Laporte,[31] who had probably asked him about the anti-Semitic and "fascist" import of some of his prewar statements that the "humanist" *doxa* took pleasure at the time in reporting, it was Blanchot who spoke of his "*detestable* lampoons" and "*detestable* words" (my emphasis)—and as such "reprehensible." (On several occasions, he also uses the word "execrable.") It is true that he points out at the same time that the offending statements—which are in effect damning—"remain without author," never having been "collected in a book." Such words are at the very least ambiguous, especially when one thinks of the "protestation" of anonymity in his *Political Writings* of the period 1958–1993.* They certainly pose a formidable problem. I will return to it as soon as possible.

* See Maurice Blanchot, *Political Writings, 1953–1993*, trans. Zakir Paul (New York: Fordham University Press, 2010); Maurice Blanchot, *Écrits politiques. Guerre d'Algérie, Mai 68, etc. (1958–1993)* (Paris: Scheer, 2003).

Annexes

1. Birth Is Death

To the memory of Sarah[1]

> Living is a death, and death is also a life.
>
> —Hölderlin, "In lovely blueness . . ."[2]

There are "primal scenes." This is known, or recognized, since Freud—at least. These scenes are matrix scenes: remembered, reworked, or reconstituted, if not quite invented, through a kind of back projection—elaborated, then—they inform or govern a *destiny*, individual or collective. A life, like a civilization, is the repetition—the "reaction," in the strict sense of the term—of these inaugural or, more exactly, immemorial scenes, if one allows the latter qualifier to mean what it should mean: they are prior to memory itself, of which they are in truth the most precise possibility—and hence impossibility: the ravage of oblivion. All existence—the *fact* of existing, or *that there is* existence—is the memory of that which, by definition, there is no memory: birth.

This scenes-mechanism, the most ancient there is, has long been demonstrated by mythologists and ethnologists: it is the mechanism of the *citation* of mythic schemata or sequences, thought as models of existence and generators of behavior. Yet one mustn't forget that the whole of classical ethics, ancient or modern—from Plutarch to Montaigne, or to Rousseau and Nietzsche—was founded on the meditation of *examples* (the "illustrious men") and that Christian ethics, which availed itself of the "life of the Saints," ended up being summarized in *The Imitation of Jesus Christ*. It is with full knowledge of the facts that the prophet of the death of God entitled his autobiography *Ecce Homo*.

It is doubtless not absurd to assume therefore that this very phenomenon is an integral part of "Literature" as such. The origin of literature can thus also be said to be immemorial. With the difference, however, that it might be said to sustain itself through a memory that is even more impossible, although it is its exact reverse, than the impossible memory of birth: the memory of death.

This is what Artaud—in *exemplary* fashion, it seems to me—could be said to bear witness to. Certainly the Artaud of the well-known "Vieux-Colombier Lecture."

Two "primal scenes" are likely to preside over the West—and its literature. Or the West *as* literature.

They were both set down [*installées*]—forever—by the Homeric poems. It is the scene of wrath (Achilles, the *Iliad*) and the scene of *experience*, literally: of the journey through a peril [*traversée d'un péril*]—a maritime term, as is known (Ulysses, the *Odyssey*). The West is wrathful and adventurous, "experimental," even when it becomes Christian and when the wrath of the biblical God (and of the prophets) comes roaring against Greek myth. Or when the destiny of Spirit, which it considers to be its Destiny—if not Destiny itself—is called the journey through wilderness [*traversée du désert*] and back: back to the self, back home (Ithaca is a Promised Land). Or: passion, death, and resurrection. "There where danger is, grows also that which saves."[3] So said Hölderlin, who saw in Kant "the Moses of [his] nation."[4] But Hegel, and Schelling, who both defined philosophy (Western thought), from its most distant origin, as "the Odyssey of consciousness," could have subscribed to the same verdict just as well. In any case, they all inherit the following knowledge from Luther: "God himself is dead." I'll talk about this again later.

The scene of wrath has to do with justice and thus with judgment: the last judgment, according to Jewish and Christian eschatology (which is not necessarily "messianism"). Artaud reenacts this scene, under the invocation of the martyr (the exemplary witness) he elected: Van Gogh, "society's suicide." This is called (not by accident, after all): *To Have Done with the Judgment of God*. Let there be no mistake: there is judgment, but to have done with judgment. The last judgment of "the Last Judgment," the end of "the reign of Ends." Artaud protests and, like Achilles (or Job), seeks redress. It is an attempt to achieve, vehemently and rebelliously (the "holy wrath"), theologico-metaphysical spoliation—the theft of the soul. Such wrath is comparable to Nietzsche's, which is just as painful, just as pathetic. But perhaps more severe. Pleas are made for dispossession and dispropriation to cease—at last. Nietzsche was jubilant; Artaud suffers martyrdom. His question is by no means: who am I? Nor even: am I still living? (Those are after all childish—and narcissistic—questions.) His question is: why was I "forced" to be? Why was I *forcibly unsensed* [forcené] (to borrow one of his own expressions)? And that is the question of death—of birth.

The *experience* of Ulysses, on the other hand, is not just one of navigation nor even of the relentless determination to return. It culminates in the journey through death [*traversée de la mort*], the descent to Hell—henceforth an inevitable *topos* for all great (Western) literature, from Virgil and Lucan to Dante or to Joyce, and to Broch. The episode, technically, is called *nekyia*: the hero steps across toward the dead—the "step (not) beyond [*pas au-delà*],"[5] as Blanchot puts it—he crosses "that shallow, calumniated stream: death"[6] (the phrase is Mallarmé's): the Styx, the Acheron. He returns. He returns, but with the aim of not recovering from his return [*pour ne pas en revenir d'en être revenu*]. For this reason, he says (he recounts), he writes: he knows that he is dead, and that is Knowledge [*Science*] itself. The myth of Orpheus means nothing else, and that is the myth of the origin of poetry, that is to say, of art.

(Do not think that at stake here is nothing but abstraction, reserved for literary or philosophical rumination [*ressassement*]. History itself obeys these scenes: de Gaulle, in 1940, was about wrath, and Mitterrand, in 1981, was a descent to the dead. The symbolic order is unfailing.)

This elementary reminder is justified only on the basis of reading Artaud's preparatory notebooks for the "Vieux-Colombier Lecture," delivered (though not necessarily "vociferated") on January 13, 1947. In one of the three notebooks brought along by Artaud for the occasion—if one can trust the transcription proposed by Paule Thévenin (on reflection, one can indeed)—one reads, suddenly, that Artaud was crucified, on Golgotha, two thousand years ago. Artaud was Christ: "God himself is dead." It is "delirium," most assuredly. Dr. Ferdière, who "treats" him, tells it to him. I quote:

> —(The following, *whispered*.)
>
> Do you know, Mr. Artaud, how one calls the delirium which consists in fancying oneself as a great historical figure by espousing that figure's individual traits?
>
> —Have you gone mad, imbecile psychiatrist, and from where did you get that I fancied myself as Jesus Christ? I simply told you, and I repeat, that I, Antonin Artaud, 50 years of age, remember the Golgotha. I remember it, as I remember being at the asylum at Rodez in February 1943, dead after undergoing electroshock treatment against my will.
>
> —If you were dead, you wouldn't be here.
>
> —I am dead, truly dead, and my death was medically certified.

> And then I *returned* as a man would return from the beyond [*l'au-delà*].
> And I remember the said beyond, too.*

The scene is perfectly framed: it is the most ancient scene, the *oldest*. Artaud comments on it as follows (and does so without making sentences, as it were, just a murmur: "no vociferating," he says):

> It was the third electroshock that caused my death.
>
> I had fallen asleep with difficulty when receiving the electrical discharge and I remember having gone round wild for an indefinite amount of time like a fly in my own throat, and then I felt myself croaking and springing up over my own dead body, but without managing to separate myself entirely from my body.
>
> I was floating in the air like a captive balloon, wondering where the road was, and whether my body would ever follow me on it [. . .].
>
> There I was, struggling, when a sudden click made me fall back to earth and I awoke in the room in which the electroshock had struck me.
>
> I found out later that Dr. Ferdière, thinking I was dead, had ordered two nurses to carry my body to the morgue and that waking up at that moment was what had saved me.†

Artaud reenacts the entire scene. In truth, he thus reenacts them all. Which means: all of the deaths. That of Montaigne, fallen from his horse (*Essays*, book 2, chap. 6, "On Practice"); that of Rousseau, who repeats it (*Reveries of the Solitary Walker*, II); that of Chateaubriand (*Memoirs from Beyond the Grave*); that of Rimbaud (*A Season in Hell*); or that of Mallarmé, declaring: "Destruction was my Beatrice"[7] and confiding in his friend Cazalis: "I can say now that I am completely and utterly dead."[8] And how many more, including the Blanchot of *The Instant of My Death*. The impossible experience of death is the *authorization* of Literature, and there is not a single writer who concerns himself with its essence who is not, from the outset, already dead. Or what else might he have to say—that is important?

To write is to say how one has died. And that is thought itself, which is not to be surprised at the fact that "I am" but to be overwhelmed by the fact that "I have no longer been." Death is like the categorical imperative of thought,

* Antonin Artaud, "[Histoire vécue d'Artaud-Mômo]" (1947), in *Œuvres complètes* (Paris: Gallimard, 1994), 26:168 [my translation].

† Artaud, "[Histoire vécue d'Artaud-Mômo]," in *Œuvres complètes*, 26:168 [my translation].

of Literature. Hegel made a system of this necessity. But Artaud voiced it [*l'a proférée*] suffering in the extreme, and that is called poetry.

2. The Agony of Religion

Since the collapse of Christendom—or, as is customary to say nowadays, of the theologico-political—two religions, in Europe, have sought to establish themselves: the religion of politics and the religion of art. This founding exigency, which broadly configures the "Modern," came to light in the last decade of the eighteenth century, shortly after Rousseau's death. Inasmuch as places have the power to emblematize epochs, this took place between the Paris of Robespierre (the Terror and the Cult of the Supreme Being) and the Jena of the Schlegel brothers (the dazzling adventure of the *Athenaeum*, through which was expressed the dream, a thoroughly Lutheran one, of an "invisible Church," if not, as Hölderlin most likely put it right around the same time, of a "Communism of spirits"). A divide, already, between nations, and a divide, already, within those nations. A fury was thus born because here and there, in one mode or another (contrary to all expectations, and in particular those of thought, which did not recognize itself in it), what was sought was nothing less than the putting to work [*la mise en œuvre*] of the Absolute, which, evidently, had revealed that it had not revealed itself. As is known today, in a world that can no longer quite tell, for its part, how it might rid itself of it, nor in whose name it might forget it, the conjunction of these two religions, announced as early as that era, has caused our century's disasters—and especially the one that, to this day, will have left us speechless. An entire civilization, which had proclaimed itself to be the one and only, saw its meaning founder and collapse therein; any "document of culture" became in effect a "document of barbarism."[1] And such was, in the case in point, the only (and disastrous) "revelation."

The most striking meeting point between these two religions was Literature, if one accepts to call the latter the language by which mankind, undergoing that language and believing to discover in it its own definition, applies itself to overcome that which subjugates it and to dictate the meaning of that which makes it exist. Thus instituting itself, Literature became Sovereignty. And it is no accident that, when it first encountered its own concept, it announced itself under the heading of a "new mythology," or that no sacralizing process was more frantic [*forcenée*] than that which affected the "senseless practice" of writing, with its endless procession of priests and sectaries, mystics and martyrs, clerics and inquisitors, accursed and apostates, soldier-monks and heretics, prophets, saints, fanatics and schismatics, blasphemers and profaners. The entire Church repeated itself in Literature, as well as all the ancient forms of worship. Literature was the madness of the dead God, even when He was believed to be alive, in one form or another.

Everything destined Blanchot to occupy this meeting point—as so many others in this century, indeed as almost everyone. But he was, more than any other, with more passion and relentlessness, more fervor and obstinacy, more magnanimity [*hauteur*] and abnegation, Literature itself. His voice—his voice alone, reduced to itself—was the Authority. It taught us Myth, in its most cruel truth: that one had to die through the work of language. Deafened, that is, still *infans*, I thus heard it for the first time, forty years ago. I was thinking, like everyone else, in terms of vocation. I entertained the hope of a community. I did not perceive that this voice, already, was expiring, nor that it was growing, already, more and more distant in the murmur in which the glare of what it had proclaimed would be veiled.

"Authority expiates itself." Who pronounced these words, Bataille or Blanchot? It is easy for us, today, under the pretext that a language of piety and purity is still at work there, to attribute those words to Blanchot as if they concealed the avowal of a mistake, of repentance, or worse: the proof, through some improbable "conversion," of an incorrigible perseverance in search of the Absolute. To do so implies not having read him nor, especially, heard him. Long before he was compelled to withdraw, since the beginning perhaps, Blanchot never ceased to suspend, in that unheard-of phrasing [*phrasé inouï*] which obstinately moves across [*scande*], and gives rhythm to [*rythme*], the humble preposition "without [*sans*]," everything that language forbade him not to affirm and not to deny: revolution and community, the work and experience, friendship and death, transparency and pain. Literature and the ordinary conversation. Since Montaigne, at the dawn of the modern, no voice has shown more restraint. Nowadays, one does not even dare to say: after the unleashing [*déchaînement*], no lesson will have so strongly undermined all lessons, no demand to have to answer for that which excludes in advance any response will have been so precisely addressed to us. The step (not) beyond [*pas au-delà*][2]—of religion: of Literature and of politics, and even of what is so emphatically called ethics. In a few rarefied texts, at the edge of an accepted silence, there still resonates, but it is no promise, the protestation of an a-theist existence that no longer even worries about the deposition of meaning but that does not give up the urgency of a task either. Who else has attempted to take this step—impossible to take?

I can still hear that "intimation," it was more than twenty years ago: "You who live later, close to a heart that beats no more. . . ."[3] Nothing was demanded. It is demand itself. One must still keep watch.

11
Ending and Unending Agony (22 September?)

Ending and Unending Agony

> I can well say that I did not begin to live until I looked upon myself as a dead man.
>
> —Rousseau, *The Confessions*, VI[1]

At the center, or very nearly so, of *The Writing of the Disaster* (1980), a relatively short text—a fragment, if you will—stands out by two distinctive features.

Printed in italics (according to a law of alternation that already for some time had presided over the composition of Blanchot's "fragmentaries"),[2] the text bears a title in roman typeface—read aloud, let's say, and with no particular intonation: "A Primal Scene"—which we come across again, several times, in the second part of the book (but whose first appearance is on page 72 [117]). In its typographical presentation, however, as in its allusive or quotational character, the title is bound to surprise: inscribed in parentheses and suspended by a question mark, it refers evidently—albeit distantly—to the phrase or analytical concept introduced, as is known, by Freud in 1914 in his essay on narcissism.[3] The title must therefore be read—if not heard—as follows: "(A Primal Scene?)."

The second distinctive feature is that the text, unlike all those—and without exception—distributed by the fragmentary, gives every indication that it is a narrative [*récit*], or at least the evocation, quite rare in Blanchot, of a childhood memory. Despite being narrated or recounted in the third person, its initial device [*dispositif*] is unambiguous (and no less so as is the device that, between the title and the narrative, and through the carefully calculated use of pronouns, overdetermines *The Instant of My Death*): without doubt, the text in question is openly autobiographical—and not simply detectable or arousing suspicion as such, as it happens in Blanchot's fictions, in certain observations or certain dialogues inserted in the fragmentaries, in a good many testimonies, not to mention (why not?) in the whole of his literary-critical work, which in the end presents itself as the autobiography of an indefatigable reader.

Now, it so happens that this text—the same text, or very nearly so*—had been published four years earlier in the fourth issue (February–March 1976) of a review—*Première Livraison*—edited by Mathieu Bénézet and myself.[4] Self-published and intended for a narrow readership, the review had as its characteristic feature a precise rule to follow: of every author we approached, whoever it was (the choice was ours), we asked for a text composed in whichever form they chose, provided it didn't exceed one typewritten page in length. We had written to Maurice Blanchot. He responded—for it was indeed a response addressed to us in return (using the enunciative device to which I was alluding just now)—with the text that concerns us here.

Allow me to read it here in this "first" version:

> *A Primal Scene*
>
> You who live later, close to a heart that beats no more, suppose, suppose this: the child—is he seven years old, or eight perhaps?—standing, drawing the curtain and, through the pane, looking. What he sees: the garden, the winter trees, the wall of a house; as he sees, no doubt in a child's way, his play space, he grows weary and slowly looks up toward the ordinary sky, with the clouds, the grey light, the drab daylight without depth. What happens next: the sky, the *same* sky, suddenly open, absolutely black and absolutely empty, revealing (as if through the broken pane) such an absence that all has always and forever been lost therein, so much so that therein is affirmed and dissolved the vertiginous knowledge that nothing is what there is, and first of all nothing beyond. The unexpectedness of this primal scene (its unending character) is the feeling of

* I don't take into account, for now, a first epistolary draft (in a letter addressed to Roger Laporte) nor an obvious allusion to the same episode in an equally autobiographical fragment of *The Step Not Beyond*: "To write as a question of writing, a question that bears the writing that bears the question, no longer allows you to have this relation to being—understood in the first place as tradition, order, certainty, truth, any form of rootedness—that you received one day from the past of the world, a domain you had been called upon to govern in order to strengthen your 'Self,' even though it was as if fissured, from the day when the sky opened upon its void." (Maurice Blanchot, *The Step Not Beyond*, trans. Lycette Nelson [Albany, N.Y.: SUNY Press, 1992], 2; Maurice Blanchot, *Le pas au-delà* [Paris: Gallimard, 1973], 9.) I would like to thank Jacqueline Laporte and Pascal Possoz, who have reminded me of these instances. [Blanchot's letter (dated September 24, 1966) to Laporte remains unpublished in the original; excerpts of it have been translated into German by Marcus Coelen in *Die andere Urszene*, ed. Marcus Coelen (Zürich: Diaphanes, 2008), 19–21.]

happiness that immediately submerges the child, the ravaging joy to which he can bear witness only by tears, an endless stream of tears. He is thought to suffer a childhood sorrow; attempts are made to console him. He says nothing. Henceforth he will live in the secret. He will weep no more.

For my part, I cannot begin, today, on this occasion, to sketch out an analysis of or a commentary on this text. It is in a sense self-evident, but there would be of course a great deal more to say or to recall: this narrative, if indeed it is a narrative, is in fact the narrative of a "negative" ecstasy (provided the qualifying adjective is read with reservations), accompanied by a revelation (the word appears in the text). The "narrative" is also supplied with what I would call an onto-atheological statement ("nothing is what there is, and first of all nothing beyond"), which, in part at least, sheds light on the title of the previous fragmentary (*The Step Not Beyond*, 1973), but it does not fail to evoke, also, in addition to a recurrent theme in Blanchot (that of the window, for example, of the broken pane or glass, even though it may well also involve a distant memory of his readings),* recognizable, almost familiar motifs: the emptiness of the sky, which in the fragmentary will later be referred explicitly to Bataille,† the "happiness" that "submerges the child" at the very moment he loses himself, or even (though it is hardly unexpected) the tears of Pascal's *Memorial*—a *secret* text, precisely, and one that was discovered only *posthumously*: "Joy! Joy! Tears of joy . . . ."[5]

I cannot therefore write a commentary on this text; I will limit myself instead to this simple remark:

If one sets aside typographical convention (nothing in fact could have called for the italics in this "first" version of 1976) and two minor modifications (a colon replaces a semicolon in the "second" version (line 3 / line 5),

* In *Faux pas*, one reads, apropos William Blake, this incidental question: "If, at the age of four, he saw God at his window, was it as a poetic genius, precociously called to break banal appearances, or did his vision express a more profound leap, a divination of another essence?" (Maurice Blanchot, *Faux pas*, trans. Charlotte Mandell [Stanford, Calif.: Stanford University Press, 2001], 31; Maurice Blanchot, *Faux pas* [Paris: Gallimard, 1943], 40.) I thank Daniela Hurezanu for providing me with this invaluable reference.

† See Maurice Blanchot, *The Writing of the Disaster*, trans. Ann Smock (Lincoln: University of Nebraska Press, 1995), 133; *L'écriture du désastre* (Paris: Gallimard, 1980), 202. [The fragment in question reads: "♦ 'The blue of the sky [*Le bleu du ciel*]' is what best expresses the emptiness of the sky: the disaster as withdrawal outside the sidereal shelter and as refusal of a sacred nature." As is known, *Le bleu du ciel* is also the title of Georges Bataille's narrative written in 1935 and published in 1957.]

which is divided into two paragraphs, while the "first" version forms a single paragraph), two major differences appear:

1. The title of the "first" version is, if I may put it this way, without reservations and has no suspensive punctuation marks.

2. The qualifying adjective "primal" in the sentence: "The unexpectedness of this primal scene (its unending character)" disappears in the "second" version, and it is not too difficult to notice, immediately, that this second difference only accentuates or even exacerbates the first.

Accordingly, what I will attempt to do is to sketch out—naturally, in a very elliptical manner—a first response to the question: what might well have happened between the two versions? What compelled the passage from the one to the other? And if I speak of a "first response," it is also because, on several occasions, whether under the same (and henceforth suspended) title or not, in italics or in roman typeface, in dialogical or aphoristic form, or even in the form of an essay, Blanchot returns to this text, in the second part of the book, as if to comment on it, as if to correct, explain, or criticize it—one might say: as if, between repentance [*repentir*] and justification, to put it entirely in suspension. Or in parentheses.

My hypothesis here is that, even while maintaining this text (almost) in full, Blanchot destroys it, in part at least, "deconstructs" it, if you will (but in a very precise sense that I will no doubt have no time to explain), or even contests or annuls it in its initial intention and reach, or in a certain effect it may produce or may have produced. And of course, he does so at the risk—even though he was, more than anyone else, well prepared against it—of a dialectical move [*opération de type dialectique*]. For this reason, and for conciseness, I will limit myself to examining only the suspension and deletion of the motif of "primitiveness [*primitivité*]." And even then, I may well not get to the end of it, supposing it were at all possible to do so.

In some ways, one could say that Maurice Blanchot wanted to *frame* this text—to say the least.

In the general scheme [*dispositif*] of *The Writing of the Disaster*, just as Blanchot later on* reworks [*reprend*], fragmenting it, an essay written two years after the text in question and published originally in *Le Nouveau Commerce* (39–40, Spring 1978) under the title, the same, as yet unsuspended title: "A Primal Scene" (which again is bound to surprise: it is an essay devoted for the most part to the Ovidian myth of Narcissus), in the same way the "prose

* See Maurice Blanchot, *The Writing of the Disaster*, 125–128, 133–136; *L'écriture du désastre*, 191–196, 202–206.

poem," if I may put it this way (though I do think one may), is immediately preceded* by the equally fragmented reworking [*reprise*] of an article that appeared only slightly after the text in question. The article, also published in *Le Nouveau Commerce* (33–34, Spring 1976), presented itself as a kind of review of Serge Leclaire's book *A Child Is Being Killed*†—more precisely, of the first text that makes up the essay collection "Pierre-Marie, or the Child." In fact, Blanchot's article was itself entitled "A Child Is Being Killed," with the addition, however, in italics and in parentheses, of the following indication: "(*fragmentary*)"—a generic category used by Blanchot since at least 1970.

Leclaire's main thesis—which stems, but with great clinical precision, from the concept of "between-two-deaths [*l'entre-deux-morts*]" elaborated by Lacan apropos Antigone in his seminar on *The Ethics of Psychoanalysis*[6]—is summarized by Blanchot as follows (and despite his extreme caution, it is obvious that he speaks with full knowledge of the facts):

> According to him [Serge Leclaire], one lives and speaks only by killing the *infans* in oneself (in others also). But what is the *infans*? Obviously, that which has not yet begun to speak and never will speak, but, more importantly, the marvelous (terrifying) child which we have been in the dreams and desires of those who are responsible for our birth and who have seen us being born (parents, society as a whole). Where is this child? According to psychoanalytic vocabulary (which, I believe, only those who practice psychoanalysis may use, only those, that is, for whom it is a risk, an extreme danger, a day-to-day calling into question—or else it is nothing other than the convenient language of an established culture), we would have every reason to identify the child with "primary narcissistic representation," which is to say that this representation has the status of an ever-unconscious and, consequently, forever-indelible representation. Hence the literally "maddening" difficulty: so as not to remain in the limbo of the *infans* and of the underside of desire, one must destroy the indestructible and even put an end to (not in one go but constantly) that to which one has not, one has never had, nor will one ever have, access: necessary impossible death [*la mort impossible nécessaire*].‡

* See Maurice Blanchot, *The Writing of the Disaster*, 65–72; *L'écriture du désastre*, 108–117.

† See Serge Leclaire, *A Child Is Being Killed: On Primary Narcissism and the Death Drive*, trans. Marie-Claude Hays (Stanford, Calif.: Stanford University Press, 1998); Serge Leclaire, *On tue un enfant: un essai sur le narcissisme primaire et la pulsion de mort* (1975; Paris: Le Seuil, 1981).

‡ Maurice Blanchot, *The Writing of the Disaster*, 67; *L'écriture du désastre*, 110–111.

In its clinical scope, this thesis is not, strictly speaking, repudiated by Blanchot. What he contests, however, but from the viewpoint of thought alone (or from that of writing, for it amounts here to the same thing), is the logic that this thesis allows and that underlies it, which is nothing other than a logic of *work* [travail], be it in a psychoanalytical sense ("psychoanalytical work," "work of mourning," etc.) or in a dialectical sense ("work of the negative" or "work of the concept"). Because death, understood as "necessary impossible," is always *anterior* (I'll return to this in a moment), there can be no practical or therapeutic "lifting [*levée*]" of this death (no "transference"), no theoretical (onto-theological) "sublation [*relève*]" of it. Immediately following the passage I quoted above, and just before a long development almost entirely devoted to Hegel and Heidegger, Blanchot adds the following (he will repeat this motif several times):

> And once again, we live and speak (but with what sort of speech?) only because death has already taken place—an unsituated, unsituatable event which, lest we become mute in speech itself, we entrust to the work of the concept (negativity), or again to the psychoanalytic work which cannot but lift "the ordinary confusion" between this first death which would be an endless realization and the second death which is called, in a facile simplification, "organic" (as if the first were not).*

In support of this contestation, in order to corroborate, as it were, and not to illustrate, his summoning of Hegel and Heidegger, Blanchot—and this is by no means irrelevant—calls upon Winnicott, whose well-known posthumous conference paper "Fear of Breakdown" had been published, also in 1975, by the *Nouvelle Revue de Psychanalyse* (11, "Figures du vide"). In this piece, Winnicott had written the following concluding "Summary":

> I have attempted to show that fear of breakdown can be a fear of a past event that has not yet been experienced. [And one sees immediately the relation that this unexperienced event might bear, in Blanchot's eyes, to the event toward which the impersonal phrase (derived from Freud) "A child is being killed" gestures.] The need to experience it is equivalent to a need to remember in terms of the analysis of psycho-neurotics.
>
> This idea can be applied to other allied fears, and I have mentioned the fear of death and the search for emptiness.†

* Maurice Blanchot, *The Writing of the Disaster*, 67; *L'écriture du désastre*, p. 111.

† Donald Winnicott, "Fear of Breakdown" (1974), in *Psychoanalytic Explorations*, ed. Clare Winnicott, Ray Shepherd, and Madeleine Davis (London: Karnac, 1989), 95;

Winnicott calls this unexperienced breakdown, which nevertheless did take place—I transcribe it here literally, as does Blanchot—"primitive agony."[7] Understood in terms of an "always anterior" death—anterior, to begin with, to any subject and to any birth ("'I' die before being born," says Blanchot later on,* and not, as Leclaire has it, "from the very moment of our birth,"[8] which repeats one or the other somewhat precipitate or mechanical proposition of *Being and Time*)—understood in these terms, then, this primitive agony is a pure *fiction*. Here I must quote Blanchot again:

> This uncertain, always anterior death—the vestige of a past without present—is never individual; likewise, it exceeds the whole (which implies the advent of the whole, its realization, the end without end of the dialectic): outside the whole, outside time, it cannot be explained, as Winnicott would have it, simply by the vicissitudes characteristic of earliest childhood, when the child, still deprived of a self, undergoes overwhelming states (primitive agonies) which he cannot know since he does not yet exist, which would happen thus without taking place, leading the adult, in a memory without memory and through his fissured self, to expect them (either desiring them or dreading them) from his life as it ends or breaks down. Or rather Winnicott's reading is only an explanation, albeit impressive—a fictional application designed to individualize that which cannot be individualized or to offer a representation of the unrepresentable: to allow the belief that one can, with the help of transference, fix in the present of a memory (that is, in an actual experience) the passivity of the immemorial unknown. The application of such a detour is perhaps therapeutically useful, to the extent that, through a kind of Platonism, it allows he who lives haunted by an imminent breakdown to say: this will not happen, this has already taken place, I know, I remember—which, in other words, is to restore knowledge as truth, and time as common and linear.†

From this series of remarks, I will limit myself—in overly condensed fashion, for which I ask you to forgive me—to drawing what in my view are two undeniably major consequences:

First of all, if there is, or can be, "agony"—and in no way does Blanchot dispute this—this agony is not "primitive." Being absolutely removed from time and from the whole of what there is, this agony does not—and cannot—take place (nor, a fortiori, can it come first); it never happens, nor

---

Donald Winnicott, "La crainte de l'effondrement," trans. Jeanine Kalmanovitch, *Nouvelle Revue de Psychanalyse* 11 (1975), special issue: "Figures du vide," 35–44.

* Maurice Blanchot, *The Writing of the Disaster*, 101; *L'écriture du désastre*, 157.

† Maurice Blanchot, *The Writing of the Disaster*, 66; *L'écriture du désastre*, 109.

can it produce any event whatsoever (in whichever sense one might understand such a term, including in the Heideggerian sense of *Ereignis*). The anteriority of anterior death, of dying [*du mourir*], or of agony, precludes any primitiveness. That is also why, if memory (*mneme*, *memoria*, *mens*, but also, though I cannot say anything about it here, *menis*, that is, wrath), since Plato or just before Plato and the metaphysical thematization of reminiscence, is nothing other than *thought* itself in its possibility, that is, internalizing appropriation [*l'appropriation intériorisante*], then anterior death—what Blanchot thus also calls: "necessary impossible death"—eludes all thought: it is *lethal*, as it were; it cannot authorize any truth (*aletheia*), any revelation, any manifestation, any coming into presence.

Such is the contention of the *incipit* of Blanchot's article on Leclaire, which opens, in *The Writing of the Disaster*, the second fragment drawn from the article:

> Necessary impossible death: why do these words—and the unexperienced experience to which they refer—escape comprehension? Why this collision, this refusal? Why erase them by making a fiction out of them that is peculiar to an author? It is only natural. Thought cannot welcome that which it carries within itself and that which carries it, except by forgetting it. I will speak soberly of it, using (perhaps falsifying) the powerful remarks of Serge Leclaire [. . .].*

Second, this muted resistance that anterior death proposes—but does not oppose, that is, in the broadly received sense of dialectical negativity—a death that is a true death, dying itself, but as that which is *impossible* (to use Bataille's term), as an experience without experience (I have spoken of this elsewhere in relation to *The Instant of My Death*)[9]—this resistance, then, proposed to thought by anterior death—a death upon which thought nevertheless rests entirely, indeed unthinkably—is that which "naturally" authorizes *fiction* (the term appears here for at least the second time), as if through an irrepressible movement: narrative, for example, myth or poem.

But one sees immediately what this means: the origin—and function—of fiction is nothing other than conceptual or therapeutic, philosophical or psychoanalytical, *work* [travail]. In the same way, fiction is a product of negativity "at work [*à l'œuvre*]." Literature, philosophy, and psychoanalysis are *organized* by the same logic. It is *logic* itself.

As absolutely anterior, however, death is no less *originary*. Certainly, nothing can divide it in a first and second death, as Hegel, Lacan, or Leclaire would

* Maurice Blanchot, *The Writing of the Disaster*, 67; *L'écriture du désastre*, 110.

have us believe (although in the case of Hegel, I'm not so sure, that remains to be seen . . .). Dying [*le mourir*] is one, and this indivisibility does not authorize any mytheme, concept, or transference. Nor any "remembering [*remémoration*]." Or to put it differently, the temporalization of death alone generates "literature"—in the sense of that which is nothing but "all the rest."

But if dying, as that which is indivisible, is not the cause of anything, if only of that "thing" which is its necessary impossibility or its impossible necessity (unexperienced experience), this does not mean that it does not authorize anything—not in that inflection of the word that gestures toward the "author" but in that inflection which entails *authority*. (You will recall the exchange with Bataille: "The experience is the authority, but authority expiates itself."[10]) If, then, I describe dying as "originary," I do so in the strict sense of the *transcendental*, that is to say, in the sense of a *condition*—a condition, therefore, of negativity, but of no possibility whatsoever. Transcendental dying [*le mourir transcendantal*], the condition of existence itself—and this is its absolutely paradoxical status, falling within the province of what I thought was acceptable to call, namely with regard to Hölderlin and his thought of the tragic, a *hyperbologic*[11]—is purely and simply a *condition of impossibility*. And to begin with, that of fiction (of literature), of onto-theo-logic, of therapy—in short, of any authorized, if not authoritarian, subjectivity.

I said "condition of impossibility": the interplay [*jeu*]—or clash [*heurt*]—of these two negativities immediately suggests the "movement," as Hegel puts it, of *Aufhebung*. Except that nothing here is negated as such—that is to say, nothing is preserved and maintained, kept or sheltered: nothing is saved, to put it bluntly. And especially not existence as life. This interplay—or clash—should be understood, rather, as an *affirmation*, though admittedly not in the sense given by Nietzsche, that is, precisely, as an "affirmation of life" (of "power"). Nor has it to do with death as "my ownmost possibility," on which the existential analytic of *Being and Time* was founded. Blanchot is perfectly explicit on this subject, and I quote him here for the record only:

> But what would the difference be between death by suicide and nonsuicidal death (if such a death exists)? The difference is that the first, by entrusting itself to the dialectic (entirely founded on the *possibility* of death, on the use of death as power) is the obscure oracle which we do not decipher, but thanks to which we sense, and ceaselessly forget, that he who has been all the way to the end of the death wish [*désir de mort*], invoking his right to death and exerting over himself a power of death—thus opening, as Heidegger put it, *the possibility of impossibility*—or believing himself to be master of nonmastery, lets himself get caught in a sort of trap and halts eternally—halts, obviously, just an instant—at

> the point where, ceasing to be a subject, losing his stubborn freedom, and becoming other than himself, he comes up against death as that which does not happen or as that which turns again (belying, as madness would, the dialectic by running its course) into *the impossibility of all possibility*.*

If there is affirmation, then, it can only be affirmation of the *disaster*—of the "empty sky." Worklessness [*désœuvrement*], impersonality, disembodiment, immemorial and endless agony: the "ravaging joy," or the "feeling of lightness" of *The Instant of My Death*.[12] The "endless stream of tears" or the silent, discreet laugh. Affirmation allows of one statement only and is addressed to the other of the self (or, let's suppose, of the Self) alone: "You are dead already. . . ." And that is called *writing*.

I quote Blanchot one last time:

> Dying means: you are dead already, in an immemorial past, of a death which was not yours, which you have thus neither known nor lived, but under the threat of which you believe yourself to be called upon to live, henceforth awaiting it in the future, constructing a future to make it possible at last, as something that will take place and belong to experience.
>
> To write is no longer to situate in the future a death that has already occurred; it is to accept to undergo death without making it present and without making oneself present to it; it is to know that death has taken place even though it has not been experienced, and to recognize it in the oblivion that it leaves behind, the effacing traces of which call upon one to *except oneself from the cosmic order*, where the disaster makes the real impossible and desire undesirable.†

The scene was thus not "primal." (And it was probably not a "scene," just as there was no "secret" about it to be kept—I will return to this another time.) Or if it was, if indeed one is entitled to consider it as "coming first," as having taken place, as having remained a (memorized) memory, it is not of the order of the *originary*. One does not recognize it "in the oblivion that it leaves behind, the effacing traces of which call" upon the *disaster*.

Does that mean it is fictional, or that it is nothing but literature?

It would indeed if it were strictly autobiographical. Which is perhaps not exactly the case. "You who live later, close to a heart that beats no more, suppose, suppose this: the child [. . .]," such is the opening of the "scene" and such is the *incipit* of the text itself, its enunciative envoi. It is a quasi-posthumous address, a kind of confiding or—it amounts to the same—

* Maurice Blanchot, *The Writing of the Disaster*, 70; *L'écriture du désastre*, 114–115.

† Maurice Blanchot, *The Writing of the Disaster*, 65–66; *L'écriture du désastre*, 108–109.

confession. This text is quite simply *confided*; it calls upon a faith and a fidelity. It is a *testamentary* text, which may perhaps not simply mean that it is a "testimony." In that, it is comparable less to *The Instant of My Death* than to the *Memorial* that Pascal, precisely, had not destroyed.

But twice you have heard, in the very evocation of the insuperable limit of thought (of *mneme*), as well as that of fiction, the word "oblivion [*oubli*]." No *commentary* has come, after the fact, to frame the *Memorial*—and the same can be said of *The Instant of My Death*: the last words. Never were they corrected, reworked [*repris*], partially destroyed or "deconstructed," in short, rewritten. What happened, then, to the *primal scene*? Why did Blanchot nevertheless keep it, that is to say, *save* it?

Perhaps, and this is my last hypothesis, if only to recall Freud's own use of the concept in his essay on the genealogy of humanity as such (the "theoretical fiction," to speak like Nietzsche, of *Totem and Taboo*, or, as Lacan would say, the only "myth" of which modernity has been capable), perhaps in order to *demythologize* it—in precise relation to the immemorial.

In an obvious echo of his political formation, Blanchot had occasionally tracked down the essence of literature in the original myth of poetic fiction—Orpheus's *nekyia*, his journey through death—and sketched out the figure of "worklessness" under the name of Eurydice: the birth of the plain song [*chant pauvre*], as that of Kafka's Josephine, but of the song nonetheless, be it "utterly other," or at any rate deprived of the charm of the Sirens' song. . . . Here, in *The Writing of the Disaster*, no Mnemosyne, no Lethe. The only mythical name that appears—given "primary Narcissism" and "the death drive"—is that of Narcissus, but it does so with the relentless determination to deconstruct this "late" and every bit "literary myth": this false myth perhaps, the devastating effects of which are even worse in our societies than those of the Sophoclean version of *Oedipus*. I won't venture to affirm, without further examination, that this accusation of that which is "false" is an implicit defense on behalf of that which is "true" (myth). Probity commands that we follow as closely and as long as possible the path that Blanchot has sought to clear or mark out: writing begins—such is its *condition*—with the effacement or disappearance of mythical names and figures, in the same way as, in politics, the "change of epoch"[13] can be said to be brewing; or, in terms of so-called life, the subject strives to withdraw, abandons itself, and lets itself be deposed [*se laisse destituer*].

The fact remains that all of this—including the anxious and doubtful retention of the initial phrase or concept: *A Primal Scene*—is placed *under the sign of the disaster.* Admittedly, "disaster" is not a *name*, but the *etymon* does not cease to resonate with it—to the point of triggering, in the first part of the fragmentary, a long diatribe against Heidegger's "etymologism."[14] You have no doubt already understood that I will leave the question here unresolved, with all of its potential implications: why is this *word*, right up to the title of the *book*—a title with such an unsettling double genitive (exactly who, what, is writing?)—why is this word, then, "saved"? If the name must disappear, what does the power or *energy* of the word still consist in? Might it still hold some kind of working power [*pouvoir œuvrant*]? Is that what we call a *term*?

Appendix

[In 1976, Malraux . . .]

In 1976, Malraux—I will stick to this version—who had just been asked by the "General"[1] during their first meeting (in 1945) the question: "How do matters stand with intellectuals?" claimed he had said to him:

> There are those whom the Résistance led to historical romanticism, and the current period should be the height of their expectations. And there are those whom it led, or who led themselves, to revolutionary romanticism, which consists in confusing political action with theater. I don't mean those who are prepared to fight to create Soviets: it's not the actors I'm talking about, but the spectators. Since the eighteenth century, France has had a school of "sensitive souls," in which, besides, women of letters have played a fairly constant role.
>
> [. . .]
>
> Literature is full of sensitive souls, for whom the proletarians are noble savages.
>
> [. . .]
>
> The situation of serious intellectuals is a difficult one. French politics has happily drawn on writers, from Voltaire to Victor Hugo. [. . .] Writers thought they could play such a role again at the time of the Popular Front. Instead, the Front made use of writers more than they had taken advantage of the Front. This scheme was very cleverly worked out, on the Communist side, by Willy Münzenberg—who has since died. But in spite of all their talk about action, something Montesquieu refrained from doing, what have these intellectuals done since 1936? Drawn up petitions.*

Whether or not he said this, it was, given the period, well judged—as is often the case with Malraux. Except that, fifteen years later (or five to

* André Malraux, *Antimemoirs*, trans. Terence Kilmartin (London: Hamish Hamilton, 1968), 89–90; André Malraux, *Antimémoires* (1967), in *Œuvres complètes* (Paris: Gallimard, 1996), 3:96.

seven years earlier, seeing that the first composition of the *Antimemoirs* dates back to 1965–1967), his own daughter, Florence, signed—and was right to do so—the "Declaration of the 121,"[2] which was not, far from it, without political and historical consequences. To say nothing of the fact that the breathtaking proliferation of speeches given at RPF[3] (or UNR)[4] assemblies, the meetings with the "General," or the "matters of national importance" not only approved policies with which it was no doubt difficult for Malraux to be in agreement but also did perhaps not justify such contempt vis-à-vis petitions and petitioners, even if the latter had become something like "professionals of political commitment." Or even if they themselves regularly approved rather dubious policies.

One thing was to foresee the gradual effacement—in truth, an effacement predetermined by the "European civil war," that is, the "philosophical war" of 1939–1945, if not of 1936–1945—of a figure that goes back two centuries. Another would have been to sketch out an explanation for it that went somewhat beyond the opposition between "political action" and "theater" (even though Malraux's televised epigones have confirmed it ad nauseam) or between "theory" and "politics." (In fact, immediately thereafter, Malraux adds: "Then there are professional philosophers. For them, Lenin and Stalin are merely disciples of Marx. [. . .] A particular kind of theory: Marx, but not Richelieu. For them, *Richelieu had no politics*.")* In what is the latest significant reflection on intellectuals—*Intellectuals Under Scrutiny*—Blanchot writes, after having recalled, in response to an article by Lyotard dating of that period in which the "silence of intellectuals"† was vociferously bemoaned, that he was not "one of those who are content to seal up the tomb of the intellectual"‡ (and the following is also the most fitting response one could have given Malraux):

> The intellectual is all the closer to action in general, and to power, for not getting involved into action and not exercising any political power. But he is not indifferent to them. In standing back from the political, he does not withdraw from it, he does not retire from it, but rather attempts to sustain this space of

* Malraux, *Antimemoirs*, 90; Malraux, *Antimémoires*, in *Œuvres complètes*, 3:96. Malraux's italics.

† Jean-François Lyotard, "Tomb of the Intellectual," in *Political Writings*, trans. Bill Readings and Kevin Paul Geiman (London: UCL Press, 1993), 3–7; Jean-François Lyotard, "Tombeau de l'intellectuel," *Le Monde* (October 8, 1983), reprinted in *Tombeau de l'intellectuel et autres papiers* (Paris: Galilée, 1984), 11–22.

‡ Maurice Blanchot, "Intellectuals Under Scrutiny," in *The Blanchot Reader*, ed. and trans. Michael Holland (Oxford: Blackwell, 1995), 207; Maurice Blanchot, *Les intellectuels en question* (1984; Tours: Farrago, 2000), 11.

> retreat and this effort of withdrawal so as to take advantage of this proximity at a distance and install himself there (a precarious installation), like a look-out who is there solely to keep watch, to remain watchful, to wait with an active attention, expressive less of a concern for himself than of a concern for others.*

I do not subscribe blindly to all of Blanchot's claims. In spite of what I may have said myself on this subject a decade ago, I am not at all sure that, as Blanchot has it, "from the Dreyfus Affair to Hitler and Auschwitz, the proof is there that it was anti-Semitism (along with racism and xenophobia) which revealed the intellectual most powerfully to himself."† Nor am I at all sure that, as he adds almost immediately, "the categorical imperative, losing the ideal generality given to it by Kant, became the one which Adorno formulated more or less thus: 'Think and act in such a way that Auschwitz may never be repeated,' which implies that Auschwitz must not become a concept and that an absolute was reached there, against which other rights and other duties must be judged."‡ I obviously cannot, in the context of this survey, go back over the onto-theological *concept* of the "absolute," which allows here for the repetition, in a sense closely related to Heideggerian *Wiederholung* (localization, nomination, historization, in a word, *finitization*), of the Kantian *categorical* imperative. I will limit myself simply to the following (which, besides, Blanchot does not fail to suspect, albeit laterally, as well): if anti-Semitism has been (and remains) de facto the fault line of this catastrophic century (as is known, it has even cut across the "antifascist bloc," which is doubtless more revealing than any phenomenon of "totalitarian" contamination complacently singled out by the new German historiography), it did not take the modern formulation of the "Jewish question" for intellectual *protestation* to manifest itself. It is essentially for having defended the memory of the Protestant Calas that Voltaire is regarded as the (noneponymous) hero of the "race of intellectuals," as one used to say at Altenburg (or at Pontigny). What's more, it is not in the least irrelevant that, well before the substantivization of the term "intellectuals," their position or function had been more or less contemporaneous with the transformation affecting the word "protestation" itself: *disapprobation*, *opposition*, *indignation*, *refusal*, etc., thus encompassing the Latin (and religious) meaning of attestation—of a belief, of a faith, of a conviction. Protestantism is seen as the symptom, if not the

* Blanchot, "Intellectuals Under Scrutiny," 207–208; Blanchot, *Les intellectuels en question*, 12.

† Blanchot, "Intellectuals Under Scrutiny," 223; Blanchot, *Les intellectuels en question*, 52.

‡ Blanchot, "Intellectuals Under Scrutiny," 223; Blanchot, *Les intellectuels en question*, 53.

agent, of the collapse of the theologico-political. Intellectual protestation, on the other hand, stems initially from rebellion against religious totalitarianism. Marx, one too often forgets, was Lutheran, and not just because he had drawn on speculative idealism. (What else was the "German revolution," at the start, other than the revival, on the basis of the French experience, of the old project of "general Reformation" that the radical Lutherans had opposed to Luther's alliance with the Princes?) That intellectuals have been construed, sometimes unkindly, as heirs of clerics is certainly not a validation of Dumézil's trifunctional hypothesis. Rather, if intellectuals have been thus construed, it is because, in their struggle against theologico-political substantialism (embodied sovereignty, from the Lord to the lord), the anger of the righteous merged with the demand for religious freedom, that is, ultimately, for freedom of thought. But this implied that faith, followed by thought, would be referred to a subject—not a "subjugate [*assujetti*]" but another substance, more readily powerful on account of its disembodiment—and that the latter, in turn, would be referred to conscience.

In the closing pages of his essay, Blanchot quotes these "words of warning" by Foucault: "For a long time, the so-called left-wing intellectual spoke, and was accorded the right to speak, as the master of truth and justice. He was listened to, or claimed the right to be listened to, as the representative of the universal. To be an intellectual was to some extent to be the conscience of all."*

Foucault speaks cautiously of "the so-called left-wing intellectual," and it is perhaps regrettable that Blanchot, who had therefore read Foucault, as well as the detailed work by Jean-Denis Bredin, did not find it necessary to make distinctions that are nevertheless called for: between intellectuals who are intellectuals by trade (teachers and scholars, writers [*écrivains*] and nonliterary authors [*écrivants*], artists, etc.) and not necessarily on account of renown, which, in constantly exposing them to the "public space," affords them de facto a political or civic responsibility that almost automatically extends beyond the space in which their trade is practiced; clever individuals ("men with ideas" who advise or support the princes, and these are always legion); ideologues; so-called right-wing intellectuals (of whom Heidegger is *also* a perfect example), etc. But Blanchot's reminder of these "words of warning" is valuable in that it allows us to sketch out the outline of the closure [*clôture*]—yes, in a Heideggerian sense—of the age of intellectuals. This closure does not close along the line that charts the breakup of universals (Reason, Progress, Humanity, the Course of history [*Sens de l'histoire*], etc.)

* Blanchot, "Intellectuals Under Scrutiny," 224; Blanchot, *Les intellectuels en question*, 56.

or the erosion of "grand narratives" (of modernity, according to Lyotard), let alone the "devalorization of all values" (nihilism). Rather, it begins to set in when conscience itself becomes problematic.

Neither Malraux nor Sartre could have questioned conscience. Even less so today's neohumanists, who have "tossed out" the "philosophies of '68," as they put it, for the sole purpose of making accessible—that is to say, of selling—that which was, academically, accessible to them: a bit of Kantianism (but certainly not Kant . . .). The only rigorous delimitation of the concept of conscience could only proceed, as is well known (Foucault, at least, knew this very well), from the delimitation of what is referred to as metaphysics, the necessity of which was inscribed in philosophy since the time when Voltaire, precisely, won fame through protestation (Kant's *Dissertation* dates back to 1770, the Calas Affair to 1765). And it is just as well known that the delimitation of philosophical humanism had to follow as an irreversible consequence. Lyotard was right to ask himself, as Blanchot reminds us,[5] in the name of which "universal victim-subject" one could still protest. And indeed, this is where we stand today, at the risk of trudging in—or parading—wishful thinking and fine sentiments—or what amounts to the same: the absence of thought, pure and simple.

All the same, this in no way undermines the necessity of protestation.

I confess that I was still tempted to detach from its context the following (and almost final) sentence of Blanchot's essay: "In this there is a moral constraint which some cannot elude, which others refuse. It is beyond all judgment."* I could have used these lines as an "epigraph." But I changed my mind: I thought—to trade off an imperative, even an exhausted one, against another—one had to keep resisting or refusing words too hastily employed or employed simply to avoid, provisionally, an improbable resolution to "revolt" [*un improbable "se révolter"*]. The delimitation of humanism promised a kind of arch-ethics, something that would carry, without fundamental or radical foolishness [*niaiserie*], the unjustifiable "moral constraint." Yet, whatever weight they carried, none of the great thoughts that ventured on this path were capable of eschewing what I shall call, for lack of a better word, fideistic subjection [*sujétion fidéiste*]: it is blatant in the mytho-theology of the later Heidegger (the Heraclitean *daimon*, at best) and no less so in Benjamin's messianism "without messianism," in Bataille's atheology or in the religiosity of the "humanism of the Other"—to mention only the departed. It seems to me, however, that protestation is such that it implies a *defiance*—and I shall add: one that is irrevocable [*sans appel*]. Or, if one prefers: it implies a

* Blanchot, "Intellectuals Under Scrutiny," 225; Blanchot, *Les intellectuels en question*, 58.

responsibility that responds to nothing (to no injunction), nor to anyone (to no call [*appel*]), a responsibility that does not even rely on the "one must [*il faut*]" that it nevertheless declares when it is confronted with the raw fact of injustice and evil—two "concepts that are rather difficult to 'determine.'"

Defiance would perhaps open up the possibility of a task for those who still accept to call themselves, without feeling too much ashamed, "intellectuals." To bluntly answer what, as I see it, is the main question of this survey: I *still* recognize myself in protestation—that is to say, above all, in the struggle against all forms of the religious and its supposedly secular substitutes: statism, nationalism, ethnicism, sexism, liberalism, or economism (since I am evidently not one of those who imagines it is possible to separate the political from the social), everything that leads to servitude and murder—the list is long. I have lent my "signature" or, depending on the circumstances and my capabilities, have done a little more when it seemed to me that it was not futile for the "one must" to become public. In this I am prepared to remain obstinate.

Interview with Pascal Possoz

I

Pascal Possoz: From 1976 to 1980, you were at the center of what might be called the "primal scene" episode: you had solicited Blanchot for the text in question.[1]

Philippe Lacoue-Labarthe: Yes, together with Mathieu Bénézet.[2]

PP: When Blanchot worked again on the question of the "primal scene" in *The Writing of the Disaster*, he occasionally quoted you for the purpose of clarifying the process; for example, when you say, quoting Schlegel, that "every poet is a Narcissus."[3] Not only, then, did you solicit a text from Blanchot, but at one point the latter also referred to you explicitly. . . . Did you exchange any letters?

PhLL: Very few. A brief word, every now and then, which never said anything of a theoretical nature.

PP: But he had read *The Literary Absolute*.[4]

PhLL: Yes, that's where he had come across Schlegel's text.

PP: And *The Literary Absolute* was itself already a response to *The Infinite Conversation* and his text on the *Athenaeum*, which had been the driving force behind your work.

PhLL: Yes, together with Benjamin's thesis. At the time it had not been translated (I later translated it with Anne-Marie Lang),[5] but we knew of it, and since Jean-Luc Nancy reads German, we knew very well what was in it. We reckoned that translating it would be a dreadful task, but we could understand it.

PP: Is there an obvious link, at the outset, between the Jena group and the appearance in Blanchot's work of the primal scene? Is there among the pre-romantics a founding element for what Blanchot sought to rework by distinguishing romantic narcissism from what he would redefine as the anti-Narcissus?

PhLL: With regard to narcissism, one cannot rule out a connection. But between Jena and the writing of "A Primal Scene," I don't think there is a direct link. And at the time, in 1976, *The Literary Absolute* had not yet been published.

PP: But he had read your work . . .

PhLL: Yes, he had, and I knew this because Roger Laporte had told me. We (Mathieu Bénézet and myself) therefore wrote him a letter—although, typographically speaking, I'm the one who wrote it—and fifteen days later, we received the text in question. He thus responded quite spontaneously.

PP: Do you think he had already written it?

PhLL: I don't think so.

PP: Was there anything unusual about the proposal you had sent him?

PhLL: Yes, we had asked for "a text that does not exceed one typewritten page in length." We had had this idea in mind for the layout of our review *Première Livraison*:[6] six times a year subscribers to our review would receive a folded sheet of paper, and at the end of the year, we'd have the sheets bound with a front cover indicating the authors' names.

PP: He knew, then, what form the review would take.

PhLL: We had explained it to him.

PP: Can one say that the review is made of fragments?

PhLL: Yes, since we solicited texts that didn't exceed one typewritten page. It could be a poem or a fragment; some chose to send in a page of prose cut off arbitrarily at the beginning and end. Everything was permitted.

PP: Had you conceived of this review with Mathieu Bénézet?

PhLL: Yes.

PP: In creating a review in 1976, was it your ambition to pursue the kind of work Bataille had done around his review? Was this ambition in some way similar to that of the *Revue internationale*?[7] Was a history of thought around the review in general at stake?

PhLL: Yes, which is also why, two years later (Mathieu Bénézet had taken care of it, and that's how I came to know Christian Bourgois),[8] a collection entitled "Première Livraison" was created in association with the review.

PP: And did a considerable number of texts appear in this Bourgois collection?

PhLL: There was a collection of poems by Jacqueline Risset, as well as a little book by Dominique Laporte provocatively entitled *Histoire de la merde*. . . . It was also in this collection that I first published my translation of Hölderlin's translation of *Antigone*.[9] And there were other publications.

PP: When did the collection fold?

PhLL: Two or three years later, when the review's venture came to an end.

PP: When Blanchot sent you his text, was it accompanied by a commentary?

PhLL: No, only a short note, along the lines of: "Here's the text I have written in response to your invitation."

PP: He therefore must have written it over a span of a fortnight?

PhLL: Yes.

PP: What was your reaction upon receiving it?

PhLL: We were overjoyed to have a text by Blanchot. Overjoyed that he had responded to our invitation and a rather imperious invitation at that: a single typewritten page, no more, for a group of people he had read and knew only by name (besides Roger Laporte, Jacques Derrida had told me this as well). He responded favorably, without the slightest hesitation, and had sent the text in question.

PP: He was thus happy to write in a review of this kind.

PhLL: Probably, or at least he trusted those who edited it.

PP: And what about the text itself?

PhLL: I was astounded at the fact that despite its quite subtle composition, that is to say, the obvious distribution, in the enunciation, between an address ("suppose, suppose this . . ."), where he alone—"me," Blanchot—can be said to be saying this, and a narrative voice in the third person ("the child—is he seven years old, or eight perhaps?"),[10] it was, to my knowledge, the first "autobiographical" text by Blanchot. As far as I know, he had never written anything like it.

PP: It thus seemed clear to you from the outset that it was autobiographical, that it couldn't have been addressed to any reader.

PhLL: Yes, certainly. It was addressed to us, the younger generation. The text basically says at the beginning: "I'm old, I haven't got long, I'm giving this to you—this memory."

PP: Did one fear he might be at death's door, as early as 1976 (he was about to turn seventy)?

PhLL: Yes. He felt he was aging.

PP: In any event, the text surprised you because it was autobiographical.

PhLL: Yes.

PP: So, first came the joy of receiving a text from him; second, the joy of receiving an extraordinary text; and third, there was a question about its content.

PhLL: Yes.

PP: What was Mathieu Bénézet working on at the time?

PhLL: He was writing poetry, and in those days had already published several collections of poems, the first of which caused quite a stir, for it was, among other things, promoted by Aragon, who saw in him much promise. It was called *L'histoire de la peinture en trois volumes*.[11] And it was a collection of poems! He had also written a sort of narrative, more or less autobiographical, entitled *Dits et récits du mortel*.[12] We had met thanks to a mutual friend who had put us in contact, and we had got on well despite political disagreements: at the time, he was still a member of the Communist Party! Yet, in spite of everything, we had decided to do something together. 1976 was still a time in which we sought to free ourselves from the yoke of avant-garde movements, such as Tel Quel and all of its avatars, in short, everything that had taken center stage in the preceding ten or fifteen years. We published two collective volumes, the first of which was called *Misère de la littérature*;[13] the second, *"Haine de la poésie"* (the latter title was borrowed from Bataille).[14]

PP: Was the review poetic in character? You had solicited a text from Jabès, another from Laporte, etc. Did you consider "A Primal Scene" to be a poetic text?

PhLL: Yes, I think it is one of the most beautiful prose poems of the century. And naturally, Baudelaire comes immediately to mind.

PP: Is it a poem?

PhLL: For me, it is, yes. But of course, when it is reworked in *The Writing of the Disaster*, it no longer has the same function. Likewise, what had been originally full-length articles, essays, or expositions were now, in *The Writing of the Disaster*, fragmented. As a result, the text had changed status, had changed its function.

PP: "A Primal Scene" therefore anticipates *The Writing of the Disaster* . . .

PhLL: Probably, since he placed it in such a way in *The Writing of the Disaster* that, even though one cannot simply say that he makes of it the center of the book (to borrow the metaphor he had once used in *The Space of Literature* when discussing the "gaze of Orpheus"), the book nevertheless gravitates a great deal around that text. And more importantly, it had since then become striking that *The Instant of My Death* was written following the same protocol: he speaks of himself in the third person ("he," "the young man").[15] As a result, for me, there are two autobiographical texts by Blanchot: this one and *The Instant of My Death*. And I recall having thought at the time: what a show of absolute confidence he is displaying here by entrusting *us*—that is, people he doesn't know, about whom he knows things perhaps only on account of what he has read of them—with a text of this kind. A text that was, at the time, a hapax in his work—there was no equivalent.

PP: It is therefore a unique text. What might have happened, then, between 1976 and 1980 that he felt compelled to write around this text? Who had read him? How had this "primal scene" been received? Had anyone, early on, produced a psychoanalytic reading of this text?

PhLL: Not to my knowledge, no. I certainly wasn't aware of any; I never met anyone who spoke to me about this text from that angle.

PP: What had you heard, at the time, from people who had read it?

PhLL: Some people very close to us (Claude Royet-Journoud, Emmanuel Hocquard, Alain Veinstein) had told us: he made you an incredible gift; one expected many great things from Blanchot, but not something like this. And suddenly the image people had of Blanchot was turned on its head.

PP: But it remained within a certain circle of people . . .

PhLL: I had very few links with psychoanalytic circles. Besides, they didn't read literature or want to hear about Blanchot, or at least weren't interested. All I can say is that at the time we had also written to Lacan, and he never responded. The only person who had spoken to me about it, but much later, was Serge Leclaire. I ought to remember the exact circumstances; I think it was around the time Jean-Luc Nancy and myself were preparing in 1980 the Cerisy conference "Les fins de l'homme," that is, the first conference organized around the work of Jacques Derrida.[16] We had solicited Serge Leclaire to take part in the conference, and in the spring, during the conference preparations, he had invited us to his country house in the Vosges. We spent an entire afternoon talking with him. He had read the text and said it had deeply affected him, and indeed, in *The Writing of the Disaster*, one notices the reappearance of a text on Leclaire, written around the same time as "A Primal Scene" and published in *Le Nouveau Commerce*.

PP: When one reads *The Writing of the Disaster*, it is impossible not to make the connection between Lacan and Blanchot (they have the same women in common, there is a community, there is Bataille, etc.), so much so that one has the impression that Blanchot had been present during the dialogue begun in 1954 between Lacan and Leclaire on the two kinds of narcissism and where the former asked the latter to work on Freud's "On Narcissism: An Introduction.". . . It is as if Blanchot had heard Leclaire talk about all this. But when, in *The Writing of the Disaster*, he speaks of Leclaire, he is in fact speaking of *A Child Is Being Killed* . . .[17]

PhLL: Yes.

PP: And when you met Leclaire in 1980, had *The Writing of the Disaster* been published?

PhLL: No, it came out in October.

PP: But had Leclaire already read the text that was in *Le Nouveau Commerce*?

PhLL: Yes, and the text did revolve around the idea of the primal scene. It criticizes the first text of *A Child Is Being Killed*, "Pierre-Marie, or the Child," and refers to Winnicott, whose "Fear of Breakdown" had just been translated in the *Nouvelle Revue de Psychanalyse*.[18] Blanchot obviously read the two texts side by side and reproaches Winnicott—but also, it's implied, Leclaire—for thinking that an actual breakdown took place, saying, in keeping with what he understands of psychoanalysis (I'm inferring this, I don't actually know) and without questioning the evidence pertaining to the breakdown: psychoanalytically speaking, the breakdown didn't take place. And this is connected to his meditation on death: I'm dead but death hasn't taken place.

PP: Just as Narcissus, who comes from a death that isn't a death and leaves traces of what hasn't taken place . . .

PhLL: Precisely.

PP: Had *The Wolf Man's Magic Word*[19] been published at that time?

PhLL: Yes.

PP: In the course of *The Writing of the Disaster*, immediately following his discussion of Narcissus, Blanchot speaks of Derrida, of writing, of the cryptic word. This entire line of thought around the crypt is thus already mapped out at the time . . .

PhLL: I think so.

PP: The crypt is cited on several occasions in *The Writing of the Disaster*. In his preface to *The Wolf Man's Magic Word*, Derrida speaks of *Death Sentence* as being the first cryptic book.[20] *Thomas the Obscure* also ends with the crypt. Does Blanchot therefore intervene here to open up this space of the crypt?

PhLL: Yes, I'm quite sure of it. *Thomas the Obscure* and *Death Sentence* are also "biographical" texts, almost in the sense given by Roger Laporte, but they are presented as fictions. This became clear to me at a later stage. Since then, Blanchot specialists have noticed that *Death Sentence* referred to the death of Colette Peignot, etc.[21] I didn't know this at all at the time, but when I read the first version of "A Primal Scene," I said to myself that *Death Sentence*, *Thomas the Obscure*, and *The Madness of the Day* all told a story.

PP: It provided a clue, in the same way as *The Instant of My Death* would do later. These are thus clues for reading the text . . .

PhLL: Yes, and I think very deliberately so. I might add, even though it is merely a detail, that a few months later I published a text dedicated to Blanchot that is a "response"—the term is quite pretentious—to "A Primal Scene."

PP: Which text is this? Where can it be found?

PhLL: It is now in *Phrase*. It is entitled "Dismay" and is dedicated to Maurice Blanchot.[22] It is also a kind of autobiographical narrative, but it begins by casting doubt on the fact that it involves a scene. And Blanchot, without spelling it out, returns to this question. There is in *The Writing of the Disaster* an apparently quite harsh allusion to literature and philosophy. He doesn't make this altogether obvious, but it set me thinking about the fact that in the final version of "A Primal Scene," Blanchot changed the title (putting it into parentheses and adding a question mark) and partly the text itself.

PP: The question mark, then, is not so much over "primal" as over "scene"...

PhLL: I think so.

PP: This also raises the question of the right you have as a philosopher to enter this metapsychological field, where a psychological event is at stake. Is this what troubles Blanchot? Legend has it that somewhere between the 1920s and 1930s, at a time that has yet to be determined, Blanchot had studied psychiatry. Roger Laporte said on France Culture that he might have even studied medicine, before withdrawing his statement.... Consequently, what's at stake in Blanchot's rewriting of this text? What's the function of the question mark that appears in *The Writing of the Disaster*?

PhLL: It is to suspend both the title *and* the thing as a whole.

PP: Isn't it also a way to authorize a commentary on it?

PhLL: The commentary comes from the question: A "primal scene"? Is that really what this is? At which point he combines his commentary on Leclaire and Winnicott (which he must have written around the same time) with reflections on fiction, as well as—indeed, I think it's all related—the whole discussion of Narcissus at the end, which is also an article that was split up, fragmented.

PP: And so the question mark intervenes, and Blanchot then frames his text with Leclaire, Winnicott, a reading of Narcissus, and an opening onto the crypt.

PhLL: Yes. It is very coherent.

PP: Why, in the context of *The Writing of the Disaster*, is there a need to make this apparent, particularly in light of the question of sovereignty, which, for Blanchot, is "nothing"? After all, it is a book that produces a physical effect. In the composition of the text, there is something that tilts the primal scene toward the nothing [*le rien*], the outside [*le dehors*], toward the writing of the disaster itself.

PhLL: Which is why I say that *The Writing of the Disaster* revolves in a sense around that text. Especially because, in my view (though perhaps I'm wrong), the question mark casts doubt precisely over the sovereignty of the author, who says: "I, Maurice Blanchot, even though I'm expressing myself in the third person, etc." All the same, it is a text that can only be read self-referentially, which still implies a kind of sovereignty of writing: the writer as sovereign. All of which he will attempt to destroy right to the end.

PP: Through the magic of the question mark, which nonetheless makes a loop and brings us back to the said sovereignty?

PhLL: Yes, but he is aware of it. The disaster can be sublime, obviously.

PP: The big question that appears in your first reaction to this is: "Was it a scene?"[23] But assuming it is a primal scene, Blanchot can be said to be describing a physiological process of psychological maturation in the development of a human being . . .

PhLL: Physiological?

PP: Physiological in that it is a key moment, at a given age, in a psychological process that reveals itself in a hectic mode, which bursts forth at that moment for the "primal scene," and which means that there is a *before* and an *after* in a given development. But it is a common process, even though it is deeply autobiographical. It becomes a crucial period in the maturation process, which may stiffen into a pathological state. Now, what happens if it does not take place? Are there primal-scene failures? If it is a primal scene, there must be a complex, a psychological space must have opened up, etc. It is a developing moment that takes place at a given time in the development of any individual. It is therefore extremely important to know whether or not it is a scene. If Blanchot thus approaches a "primal scene," it is because he is drawing near the function of the mirror . . .

PhLL: Yes, it is what he spends his time destroying in all the remainder of the book. Including the secret. For "A Primal Scene" ends by saying that he will keep the secret. But how many fragments are there to say that the secret is nothing, that there is a secret only because everyone knows what it is! I had the impression, after the event (that is, after having read *The Writing of the Disaster*), that the gift he had bestowed upon us was the following: "I'm telling you the secret." In other words, something like: "There you have it, that's what happened, and for me, everything comes from there. . . ." A rather traditional figure, then: there is a matrix scene, along the lines of: "I'm on the verge of death, you're younger, I hand this down to you." And then he comes back to it and says: "No, that didn't happen, that never happens, there is no secret . . ."

PP: Yet this primal scene can nevertheless be found in other authors. If it speaks from one's inmost depths and if there is a reception for it, it is because, in spite of everything, it vaguely indicates a period in our development that had not been named before. I was troubled to see that Jung describes the same thing: he leaves his house, goes to school one morning, he is eleven years old, and bang! it just opens up like that. And from then on, he does nothing but brood on that opening and express it. Strangely, the same scene can be found in LSD creator Albert Hofmann: he is in a garden, almost à la Rousseau, and, coming into contact with the outside, is taken by ecstasy. And his whole life will be spent trying to recover this process through substances.

PhLL: Ecstasy, precisely. And it is of course something very often evoked, if not described, in mystical literature, in poetry.

PP: But there's nonetheless a general process involved.

PhLL: Yes. Except that even in the first version, Blanchot says: ecstasy before nothing.

PP: The fact remains that Blanchot bursts here into a metapsychological field. Would you agree?

PhLL: Yes.

PP: And it is a poetic text, it belongs to literature . . .

PhLL: It is also a mystical text.

PP: Yes. It is the mysticism of negative theology. . . . But we are nevertheless in the fictional domain. And then, suddenly, we move into real life.

PhLL: But in the mode of a caesura. Since it describes *the* caesura—of his existence.

PP: I would nonetheless like to shift the weight of the question toward the "primal" aspect. I could easily see why one might criticize the notion that it is primal in that it took place before and that this primal scene is really only a secondary scene or a representation of a scene that has already taken place and that, from a psychoanalytical perspective, is sought in primary narcissism or in earlier, pre-Oedipal stages . . .

PhLL: In other words, Winnicott's childhood agonies. That's why Blanchot paid particular attention to that text. Saying, in substance, that it didn't take place—because there is no memory, no recollection of it—it wasn't lived in the strict sense, yet it took place nonetheless, as if *after the event*. In fact, the writing of this text is a perfect example of an after event [*un exemple parfait d'après-coup*]. Especially when formulated as: "nothing is what there is, and first of all nothing beyond."[24] A seven- or eight-year-old kid doesn't think there's nothing and nothing beyond! One has to have read the whole of Heidegger, the whole of Bataille, in order to formulate things in that way. Naturally, it is a phenomenon of the after event [*un phénomène d'après-coup*]. Of course he borrowed Freud's phrase, but I think that in the first version he was aiming, in a very striking way, at something where "primal" admittedly recalled psychoanalytical terminology but meant first of all: this is the originary scene of my writing.

PP: Did you think of it immediately in this way?

PhLL: Immediately. Thus: "There you have it, that's my secret, I give it to you." And "henceforth he will live in the secret"[25] means: "Everything I have ever written was a way to keep this secret." It was a kind of avowal or confession.

PP: It was his inspiration . . .

PhLL: I think it was his primal inspiration, and that he then comes back to it and says: "No, that's not what I meant to say." And that compels him to borrow the conceptual phrase "primal scene" and rework it.

PP: Which nevertheless implies that he wants to make a general process out of it.

PhLL: Yes.

PP: Allow me therefore to venture a personal question: why are you interested in this text?

PhLL: Because it strikes me that I have undergone the same experience several times, and that for me, it is indeed primal.

PP: In other words, you subscribe to it . . .

PhLL: I subscribe to it, provided that implies I'm also subscribing to Blanchot's deconstruction of the expression "primal scene."

PP: This event therefore took place in your case.

PhLL: It took place, perhaps without taking place, perhaps reconstructed after the event. . . . I'm entirely convinced by the logic of the after event [*la logique de l'après-coup*]. At any rate, when I received the sheet of paper with his text, it touched me deeply, immediately. For the text in question was sent to me; we had written down both our addresses, but he had sent it to me. I remember very well when, one morning, in January, I came across it: Blanchot's small handwriting on the envelope . . .

PP: You therefore have the text in your possession?

PhLL: I have the manuscript; it is a typewritten page with one or two corrections. I recognized something. It has been on my mind for so long; I cannot get rid of it! I have written the entire first section of my book,[26] but on the question, precisely, of the said deconstruction, on the text as it stands in *The Writing of the Disaster*, I'm having difficulty writing. I have worked on it in seminars, spending a year on *The Writing of the Disaster* and *The Instant of My Death*.

PP: On Blanchot's work as a whole and on this text as a key unlocking it?

PhLL: Yes. And on the concept of experience.

PP: If we accept for a moment that it is a primal scene, why then does Blanchot introduce Narcissus in this context? Does it suggest that this "primal scene" is an engagement with a representation, an image, a reflection, the mirror, something that compels him to launch into *The Writing of the Disaster*, essentially saying: "I know full well they will say it is narcissism, but people say it at every opportunity; fine, let's talk about narcissism, then—but which narcissism is at stake here?"

PhLL: I think that sums it up; I also think he is replying to the kind of cutting remarks, whether made tacitly or expressly and spitefully, that go along the lines of: "Well, the great self-effacing writer who disappears, who is anonymous, etc., is really only a stunt that reinforces the figure of the author, the writer as a sovereign self."

PP: It is similar to what he says of asceticism, which, he argues, could be considered as a kind of feeble way of affirming oneself by annulling oneself. And he says that it is a consequence of the vertiginous Western tendency that links misfortune to the same [*qui rapporte le malheur au même*].

PhLL: Those cutting remarks could be found admittedly not in Genette but certainly in the people around him. And this ends up producing rather crude statements like those of Todorov on Blanchot—that is, somewhat ironic statements, saying, first, "it isn't rational, it makes no sense," and then, "he is playing the self-effacing-author card, but really it only reinforces his status as an author in the romantic sense."

PP: Did this not follow a conversation with Lacan?

PhLL: No. I don't even know if they ever met. He read him, of course, and very perceptively in my view.

PP: Let's delve further into the necessity of this question about Narcissus: it involves a questioning of the image and the mirror, which can be said to represent this very peculiar perception of what takes place at that moment. Blanchot therefore returns to Narcissus in a very illuminating fashion, for the Narcissus he describes practically recalls the figure of the autistic [*la figure de l'autiste*]. In Ovid, as Blanchot explains, Narcissus doesn't speak, doesn't let others touch him, doesn't know himself: he doesn't allow others to approach him, he has no relationship with the outside world and no relationship with speech since the only words he hears are the repetition of the last word he uttered. That on which Blanchot insists here is that Narcissus doesn't know himself and cannot construct selfhood. It is a terrible verdict. Narcissus takes the shape of the in-between [*la figure de l'entre-deux*], which cannot become human and, to a certain extent, isn't born—and therefore won't die either. And if he isn't born, it is because this primal scene is the event of a birth.

PhLL: Yes.

PP: If Narcissus, who doesn't know himself, is tied up with the "primal scene," it is because the "primal scene" allows one, as is the case in Legendre,[27] to understand narcissism as the only possibility to singularize oneself, therefore to differentiate oneself from the other. Narcissus is differentiation. It is a process that allows one to step out of that which is common and arrive at the "self." It is thus a fundamental time. However, Blanchot doesn't tell us whether or not it is a nonobjectal originary Narcissus—the primary narcissism that Freud put forward in order to differentiate himself from Jung: it is not the Great Whole, it is not the Great Self, it is not the Great Transcosmos . . .

PhLL: It is the death drive! Blanchot says as much. *The Writing of the Disaster* can also be viewed as a great book on the death drive, up to and including its appendix, which is *The Instant of My Death*.

PP: But if one tries to reason as a metapsychologist, one might wonder whether he is not in fact speaking of a tertiary narcissism.

PhLL: A completely reconstructed narcissism . . . in the form of a fiction?

PP: If we take nonobjectal originary narcissism as a starting point, wouldn't Blanchot's "primal scene" be a return to a scene that could never have arisen before (since I'm in the water and don't have the information of the image), which is after all a representation, an image inside a certain presence, inside a certain event, an event that took place long before? Doesn't this ultimately provide, at a given moment in my development, concreteness to an image of something I couldn't see beforehand?

PhLL: That's what I call making a fiction out of it—a figuration.

PP: As a result of a revelation, the scene would thus be nothing other than the palpable perception, at last, of a lived experience inside the uterine liquid, that is, in the aqueous environment, in the oceanic feeling?

PhLL: Yes, but if indeed he takes this up, Narcissus—already in Freud—faces the aqueous environment as a mirror [*glace*], in every sense of the word;[28] he does not enter it. The other question I was asking myself, even before you spoke about it, was that, although I entirely appreciate that Freud says primary narcissism is preobjectal, the myth of Narcissus is secondary, given that there is an object—that is, his face: he sees something. He doesn't know it is his own face but his gaze is fixed on something objectal: a reflection.

PP: Except that it is a liquid.

PhLL: Yes, but it is a liquid that shimmers; it is not a liquid in which one can penetrate.

PP: In the mirror stage, the forming of the image is secondary to the fact of presenting myself to the mirror. There is therefore a mirror. But what I find interesting in Blanchot's primal scene is that there is an image and *then* one looks for the mirror; in other words, I know there is a mirror only through the image, through a hallucinatory effect. And these images on mirrors are represented on several occasions: in the said text, "the drab daylight without depth"[29] presents an image that prompts me to look for the mirror. At a given moment of my development, the mirror is no longer a mirror [*glace*], but there are moments when I see myself and wonder from where I'm seeing myself. As for secondary narcissism, which is a process generally identified as being absolutely essential to mankind, as being the very matter of mankind, it is an ongoing process with which one has to battle all the time. Except during this "primal-scene" moment in which there is perhaps an escape from this scheme, since it is also the age of a calling [*l'âge de la vocation*]. For Blanchot, it opens up his literary space, but one can also argue that it is a moment of private communion, the moment in which the answer given is: "God"; it is roughly the time in which one's grandparents die, the time therefore of the death of the other.

PhLL: The passing of generations . . .

PP: There is a founding moment at that age: it is the age of reason. If it is a secondary narcissism, then the "primal" scene would be really primal. As a result, it wouldn't be simply the repetition or representation of something but a scene happily lived, for the sole effect of a shattering [*bris*], of a break [*brisure*].

II

PP: The difficulty I'm always faced with is that, with Blanchot, we have an author who wrote without referring to a prior system of knowledge or discourse. He is not a philosopher, he is not a metapsychologist, he is not a man of letters. Hence the difficulty in broaching the discussion. As a result, how are we to read him? A metapsychologist might chuckle, for example. Alternatively, Blanchot is the absolute master and remains untouchable. I noticed your reaction to the reception of "A Primal Scene" in our first interview; you said it enabled you to understand Blanchot, but your reasoning didn't consist in saying, from the outset, that it was a primal scene of the psychological apparatus.

PhLL: Yes, even though I appreciate that there is a reference to Freud, to the psychological apparatus, and to what Freud called a "primal scene."

PP: I have read your text "Dismay," and it seems to me important that you dated it "Summer 1976–Summer 1981." Which is to say that you wrote it between the reception of "A Primal Scene" and the time in which you read *The Writing of the Disaster*.

PhLL: That's about right.

PP: In *The Writing of the Disaster*, Blanchot speaks of "A Primal Scene" as if he himself were surprised at this text, the latter being apparently a kind of inspiration to which he returns.

PhLL: Yes, he is surprised at it.

PP: In fact, Narcissus comes as Blanchot's immediate defense against something else: "people can always say to me that it is Narcissus, etc." But Narcissus isn't fundamentally the center of "A Primal Scene," which is either the sheer outside [*le dehors complet*] or the crypt. . . . Personally, I don't know how to hold a discourse on this. When I try to assume the viewpoint of a metapsychologist, for instance, I fail; it becomes vertiginous.

PhLL: There are two distinct problems here. There is the problem posed by Blanchot's text itself, which escapes any overdetermination by one or the other positive science. Whether he is writing on Marx, or drawing on Heidegger, or on Levinas, or, as is the case here, on Leclaire and the myth of Narcissus, one cannot say which kind of discourse is at stake. And all of it is fashioned in such a way as to make it impossible for us to say which discourse is at stake. That's what produced such a tremendously intimidating effect. All those who have approached Blanchot have had the impression of being engulfed or swallowed up by Blanchot's text and thus of being condemned to Blanchotize on Blanchot [*blanchotiser sur Blanchot*]. Up until now we have seen nothing but pastiches. Except for Bident, who has had the courage to write a biography,[30] thereby taking a rather difficult course. Everything else is like the end of *Tristan and Isolde*. . . . That's the first problem. Another problem is to be aware, for one's own sake, of the mastery one has over a given field, which Blanchot may at times broach or the propositions of which he may allow himself to be dictated by. Clearly, the text by Leclaire greatly affected him. He knew a thing or two about it, he even read the French translation of Winnicott's text, he figured it revolved around the same question; all the same, he wrote something about it. Consequently, from the moment he discusses it, it seems to me legitimate to discuss him (and the same goes for when he writes on Marx—in fact, I'm currently working on what he wrote on the latter: "Marx's Three Voices,"[31] among other texts). For a long time, Blanchot's status was that of a "literary critic" and, before that, of a "book reviewer." During his entire extreme-right-wing prewar period, and later at the *NRF*, etc., he wrote book reviews, most of the time on very specific books. He never wrote idly, "just like that," like Poirot-Delpech, for instance, in *Le Monde*. He wrote no doubt as a literary critic, but without ever referring to any particular positivity. For example, he went through structuralism without caring a damn about it; Barthes could keep on writing, Blanchot just continued in his own style; it didn't have the slightest impact on him—in short, he wasn't affected by it. The fact remains, however, that the moment he takes a step toward a determined field, the field in question may reasonably react.

PP: But coming (as I do) from one of these fields, opening up "A Primal Scene" in view of what we have been discussing, seeing that it isn't there just by chance and that it has a stake in the metapsychological field, one also realizes that there are other notions one can more or less understand or sense but that don't belong to that field and are part of the a priori position of Blanchot's reading. Yet one cannot account for everything; it's just overwhelming. And aggravating.

PhLL: Up until now Blanchot's work has given rise to only two kinds of readings: either plainly hostile readings in which it is argued that his work embodies an outmoded idea of literature (Braunrot and Todorov going so far as to quote expressly a sentence from 1938—one that, besides, is no more anti-Semitic than other similar sentences—and saying that these kinds of people belong to the past, that one might as well forget them) or readings entirely subservient to Blanchot. I, for my part, think it is also possible to say that what's at stake is a text, that it must be read as a text, even if that implies being "critical" at times. One needn't take everything literally, or accept everything, or consent to everything. For instance, it is clear that "A Primal Scene" is a magnificent piece of fiction. Blanchot was very surprised at having written such a text; he doubtless said to himself: "Why did I let that slip?" He sent us his text in an ill-considered gesture, and it compelled him to reflect on it, wondering whether or not he had invented it. And since he was a tireless reader and received his books chaotically, he leafed through Leclaire, came across the text in question, and thought to himself that it was closely related to the subject at hand. At that moment, the *Nouvelle Revue de Psychanalyse* published the article by Winnicott, who seemed to think that a real breakdown does take place in each child, at any event in psychotic cases. And so Blanchot says: "No, that's an old trick!" He had read Lacan, he had read the work done on Freud in the wake of Derrida, he knew very well that the after event [*l'après-coup*] had become the dominating category in readings of Freud, that every time Freud assigned a real origin to such-and-such event (recurring especially in the ontogenetic or phylogenetic history of a given being), people, in the wake of Lacan, would say: "Careful, it isn't real, it is a fantasy constructed after the event." For example: the father isn't a father *when* he is killed; he becomes a father only *after* he is killed. Or: the primal horde never existed as such; it is a dream, projected onto the past, of a humanity that is already humanity, etc. Blanchot was thus aware of all of this and fully appreciated that it had to do, philosophically, with the problem of the real event and of the constructed or reconstructed event. He didn't want to pursue the logic governing the fantasy because he was wary of anything amenable to the imagination, etc.—a distrust he inherited from phenomenology: from Heidegger. As a result, he thoroughly developed and thematized a kind of scenario that goes something like this: "It took place without taking place—and the proof that it took place is that I wrote it." Which, besides, is what Blanchot has always said: the "it is written" is what gives sanction. I think he thus took a detour, perhaps by accident, since, as I mentioned earlier, books just arrived randomly at his home (but he was well read enough that he could appreciate what was at stake and make something out of it). And here one has to go back to Blanchot's texts as they first appeared and see the extent to which they were conceived as articles (in this case, for *Le Nouveau Commerce*),[32] while in *The Writing of the Disaster*, one has the impression that one is dealing with juxtaposed fragments. As for Narcissus, I'm convinced that what he wanted to destroy is, quite simply, the conventional conception of narcissism. As if Narcissus presupposed a constituted self, looking at itself. . . . Instead, Blanchot says that it presupposes it to such a small extent that it is rather a dislocation of the subject even before any possible birth of a subject.

PP: There is nevertheless a sentence in which I may perhaps find a foothold: "I could die." The event having taken place, I'm confronted with such a powerful sideration—everything is so present, so there, so . . . "there is" [*tellement "il y a"*]—that I cannot quite see what's left to live. It is as if I had reached the Holy Grail: I can die.

PhLL: It is the equivalent of the "extraordinary feeling of lightness"[33] described in *The Instant of My Death*.

PP: Similarly, I have also had an experience of drowning, for instance, where I told myself: why not? Everything was *there*; it was aesthetically very beautiful; to die in the Aegean Sea appealed to me. . . . Some work perhaps needs to be done on this, for I think it was you who at the end of "Dismay" introduced the "I could die" motif,[34] which is taken up by Blanchot in *The Writing of the Disaster*. As far as my own work is concerned, I thus see two major lines of inquiry: either something along the lines of "Behind the scenes [*Les dessous de la scène*]," or starting from the "I could die" question.

PhLL: It is no doubt best to start from the "I could die" question, as *you* have things to say about that.

PP: Indeed, I could engage with it from a medical perspective. The problem is to restrict the discussion to something in particular, so as to explore other leads regarding the question of the crypt, etc. Well, we are far from having dealt fully with Blanchot, and we cannot discuss him in general terms without exposing ourselves to the question: "What's this got to do with him?"

PhLL: Yes, but one could always have said that about him, except when considering him simply as a literary critic, in which case one could say: "It's got to do with him because this is his field." He had written a few narratives. But at a certain point Blanchot withdrew completely, and I think there was a specific time in which that occurred. It goes back a long way, but in times past, he talked politics. And after that, he limited himself to literary criticism, which I think was a kind of asceticism, involving also a political asceticism.

And then suddenly, he set off again availing himself of a discourse that, although not technically a philosophical discourse, had a somewhat similar position—that is to say, a very general, very affirmative discourse: "I, Blanchot, say that this has such-and-such a meaning, that this is how it works or how it works without working, etc." I think that from that point on, one is entitled to take him literally and say to him: "Oh I see, that's what you are saying on the primal scene, on originary breakdown in Winnicott, on narcissism via a radical rereading of the myth of Narcissus; you are raising issues no one had raised before, etc." What you were saying in our first interview is true: Narcissus is autistic. I have never heard anyone say that. Even during the time in which I was working on Reik,[35] on the echo, on obsessive melody, and when I had extremely sophisticated, Derrido-Blanchotian students who were doing astounding work on the nymph Echo, etc., no one had ever come to me and said: "Narcissus is autistic." These were people who at the time were following psychoanalysis seminars given by Israël[36] or Safouan;[37] all the same, they didn't see it. Yet I think this is extremely important, especially regarding Blanchot. Basically, he was at the very edge of this, and it throws new light on Blanchot. For, in spite of all his efforts (along the lines of: dispossession, passivity, I'm the author of nothing, it is not me who is speaking, etc.), if there is anyone who carries authority, in every sense of the term, it is Blanchot. Until one realizes: but after all, he is just at the edge, he is *borderline*,[38] he is at the limit. And that's when it becomes interesting. I think it would be worthwhile here to work on something I would in no way be capable of doing, nor anyone I know: it would involve rereading the text on Narcissus and locating every instance where, from the viewpoint of clinical pathology, he says something no one had noticed.

PP: In other words, to try to give a medical reading of Blanchot?

PhLL: Yes, and all the more so as he was haunted by physicians in his narratives.

PP: Indeed, one has the impression, in the end, that he is addressing physicians.

PhLL: That's right. You see, no one had ever noted that. And the challenge, as you just put it very well, is the following: "I, as a physician reading Blanchot, have come to notice that he is addressing—or may possibly be addressing—the physician in me."

PP: I have always read him with medicine in mind. That's why I have always pressed Roger Laporte to provide the factual confirmation that Blanchot studied medicine or psychiatry. In Blanchot's narratives, there are physicians and epidemics . . .

PhLL: There are diseases, as well as all the 1930s metaphorical discourses associated with medicine. And there are also references to what was being said at the time about the camps: that they are all dying from typhus and that gas was being used to delouse them. All this metaphorical language of [inaudible][39] the medical manipulated by the Nazis must have left its mark on people.

PP: Yet there hasn't been a medical reading of Blanchot . . .[40]

PhLL: None whatsoever. There is also a passage on cancer in *The Writing of the Disaster*,[41] and I have always wondered whether he had written it before or after having read Susan Sontag, who had had a cancer and had written a book on it.[42] One would also have to reread a much earlier text by Blanchot on Thomas Mann's *The Magic Mountain*.[43]

PP: We could continue this in writing, if you agree. Although I hesitate at the dialogic form [*la forme de l'entretien*], which interests me but—

PhLL:—but we risk Blanchotizing, especially in light of the opening of *The Infinite Conversation*.

PP: Returning now briefly to Narcissus. If I talked about physiology earlier, it is because I wonder whether there is a Narcissus complex. The fact that the image can never efface itself, the fact that no image can ever represent itself, the fact that one doesn't take into account any other kind of mirror [*glace*], etc., means that the process whereby this sensation is revealed is never carried out, and as a result people remain trapped in psychosis. This can go very far: it is autism, pure and simple.

PhLL: It reminds me of Joyce's sentence regarding the thin, "transparent sheet" that separates *Ulysses* from madness. I think Blanchot quotes it somewhere, not without a certain awareness of what it implies: "I'm writing, but at the limit." I know full well that it is crude to resort to biography, but even so: Blanchot withdrew shortly after 1968, a withdrawal that had by now lasted for more than twenty years, and practically, he no longer addressed anyone, except through intermediaries, through texts, indirectly. And I note that he gradually broke off relations with everyone and did so very violently. I should add that to associate "A Primal Scene" with the reflection on narcissism is also a way to return to the immersion and oceanic feeling of *Thomas the Obscure*.

PP: Nevertheless, in *The Writing of the Disaster*, the most important thing is the "nothing beyond."

PhLL: Yes.

PP: If indeed there is an effacing of the image and one replaces it with another image, we are done for. For, to dispose of the other image . . . well, good luck! Regardless of which image. In fact, it is an experience of dematerialization, of dedifferentiation. It is a dedifferentiation enabling redifferentiation. It is a very dramatic event.

PhLL: Which is of course why Blanchot said spontaneously "scene." You are quite right, then, to say "dramatic."

PP: But in relation to the event itself, what I recall from previous discussions we have had is that, in deciphering this "primal scene," you yourself are in search of an event that took place for you personally when, at the age of four, you stepped out of your home and saw a dead soldier lying at your feet. What has always struck me is that, contrary to this scene, the feeling in Blanchot's "primal scene" is one of joy. Is there not, in the precociousness of what you present as an absolute break introduced by a world that opens up differently at that moment, an overwhelming event concealing the reality of another scene?

PhLL: Yes, no doubt.

PP: I'd like to insist on the fact that the scene is characterized by joy: "its endless trait." Indeed, the surprise, the secret, is that it is joyous and that something is taking place in a joyous atmosphere: the stream of tears, the happiness.

PhLL: It is catharsis itself: the fact of being relieved by death. That's all it is. And it happens again during that moment in 1944: the incredible "feeling of lightness."

PP: But it is also a revelation.

PhLL: Yes.

PP: It is a revelation of revelation itself, but the impression is also that it is a revelation *for* revelation as such and that there is no revelation, just its vertigo.

PhLL: It always made me think spontaneously, when reading it, of Hegel's words: "What is revealed is precisely this: that God is the revealable."[44] The revelation means nothing else.

PP: In other words: "standing, I falter." It is the vertigo of knowledge.

PhLL: But it is knowledge nonetheless.

PP: What, in the end, is the tain of this mirror? Something must take place on another kind of mirror. It is "the drabness without depth," which is suddenly a mirror of its own existence. It is a true mirror, a quicksilver mirror that manifests its presence only through its own reflection. After all, it is also Legendre's view on Narcissus, where the mirror is fluid.

PhLL: There is a mirror, but . . . without the tain.

PP: The mirror [*glace*] doesn't produce the same effect, because of the materiality of the mirror. What's needed is transparency becoming transparency via a simple but formidable break, since it happens "as if through the broken pane."[45] It is an interpolation within my myopic gaze: "the drabness without depth" that will make up my life. It is the joy of endless liberation, as in the injunction: "Free me from the too long speech [*la trop longue parole*]."[46] It is the same sensation of liberation.

PhLL: Which is why I speak of catharsis. And at that moment, it is a scene.

PP: It is a joy that isn't contagious and that cannot be shared, a joy without words bringing tears without end. Is it an experience based on lofty solitude, freedom, and being-alone [*être-seul*]? And perhaps on being-thrown [*être-jeté*]? With no secret except for something unnamable that can perhaps be translated as kindness [*bienveillance*] . . .

PhLL: Goodness [*bonté*], in any event.

PP: Goodness? At any rate, it is the scene of a break, a splinter, an effacing, a revelation on those mirrors of the fluid world in which we make images of ourselves [*nous nous imageons*], alone.

PhLL: So there is nothing.

PP: It is what I had seen in Legendre's *Dieu au miroir*: differentiation, singularization. . . . Which allows us to return to Narcissus, except that Blanchot speaks of Narcissus in *The Writing of the Disaster* in order to conclude that it is not Narcissus but the anti-Narcissus: "The poet is Narcissus to the extent that Narcissus is an anti-Narcissus."[47] And "anti-Narcissus," that is still something.

PhLL: It is too much! I mean, it is too dialectizing.

PP: Except that it is a concept. Of which I hadn't been aware. There is an article by Francis Pasche—"L'anti-narcissisme"—that describes it,[48] in particular the question of negativity. In any event, is not all of this but an opportunity to open up the crypt and enter the space of the crypt?

PhLL: Yes. I will also have to pass on to you the postgraduate work of a Romanian student who now teaches in the United States and who, without quite engaging with what you are referring to, establishes two interesting connections: the first relates to the episode of the broken glass crushed into the narrator's eyes in *The Madness of the Day*; the other relates to an autobiographical passage by William Blake in which he recounts having seen God at the window as a child.[49] It is a window episode.

PP: That would amount now to three other "primal scenes"—Jung, Hofmann, and Blake. Quite a number. How about you? Did you become a philosopher at the age of eight?

PhLL: No. I never became a philosopher.

Dismay

To Maurice Blanchot

In der lydischen Tonart[1]

—And it wasn't a scene?

—No. At least I don't think so. Not quite. But I'm also aware that it is doubtless beyond my power to explain it. I could say at most (and I'm thinking of what the question implies): it was too compelling [*trop y forçait*], far too compelling. Or, but it certainly doesn't amount to the same thing: the failing [*défaillance*] was too severe [*grave*], obviously; I no longer had enough strength. Yet, even if this were accurate [*juste*], it would be insufficient, and it would be best to try to remain silent, something to which until now I had, for my part, consented. With no regrets (it is not that important, and for other reasons, I am quits). Without betrayal either: it quite simply cannot be told.

. . . .

—No, rather, it would be that which made me say in the first place: *there is no secret, but that remains unavowable*. In the same way, and I am absolutely sure of it, it isn't a question of memory: I have forgotten *nothing*. At any rate, the failing came before.

[. . .]

—Yes, if you like: inenarrable, unavowable, unforgettable. But I shall add: the worst was the infinitesimal deterioration of it all. The degradation, yes: the weakening.

. . . .

—[. . .] On the other hand, I admit, it no longer concerned me. It is true that I was speaking. (That night, I didn't stop speaking and—I imagine it is related—being cold, and trembling; all of which, besides, were predictable, expected, if not altogether induced manifestations.) But it is also quite clear that I didn't want to say anything; I didn't address anyone; I didn't utter a single sound. I was speaking without speaking. Or rather I was listening. I'd be tempted to say: I was listening to myself, had this inexhaustible speech [*intarissable discours*] (which, besides, I had no means of interrupting, and which, I think I can guess why, was actually the clearest indication of my powerlessness or my lack of energy) not been precisely inaudible—"without voice"—and had I been able at the time, or were I able today, to rid myself of the confused, disconcerting impression that deep down, inside me, it wasn't quite I who was speaking. Nor, I hasten to add, an "other."

[. . .]

—Under these conditions, the whole affair was almost devoid of reality. (Come to think of it, the experience [*épreuve*], at times, seems incomprehensible to me.) But however much this—that is, this *speech* [discours] (you see, I'm keeping to it)—resonated *silently*, from afar, or even from nowhere or from an indeterminate elsewhere—within me outside me—there was nonetheless, in what no longer quite belonged to me as *my* head or *my* throat (assuming I have ever had, with any certainty, the feeling of such belonging), a precise journey [*trajet précis*] I'd readily identify, somehow or other, with the passage, between the neck and the larynx, from thought to enunciation: at that elusive, probably nonexistent moment, removed from time, when, from the back of the throat, *thought* (what other word to use?) takes on a kind of intangible consistency—I shall say, roughly: *takes a breath* [prend souffle]—and comes to merge with the act of expiration in which it seems to me it doesn't dissipate but simply changes [*s'altère*], and in changing, articulates and inflects itself into a vague, atonal song—in any event something scarcely melodic, something "plain [*pauvre*]" (if not altogether null), but set more or less to the rhythm of breathing. Or of something more primitive still, a beating [*battement*], I don't know.

. . . .

—And they were, yes, sentences [*phrases*], coherent propositions, but of a very general nature, rather abstract and, for me, enigmatic: not obscure, not in the least, but with no rigorous links between them, despite the staggering accumulation of logical constructions [*étais logiques*] or the somewhat hollow rigidity of the grammatical framework. They were, let's say, *spaced apart* [espacées]. Pure syntax, pure parataxis. Like snatches of a speech entirely laid out but for the best part kept tacit.

[. . .]

—Perhaps responses, indeed, sketches of responses. Yet, although it had seemed to me on several occasions that I was being subjected to some sort of cross-examination or at least that I had to exonerate myself, the questions were almost never formulated. The fundamental question around which all of it should normally have been organized was, at any rate, I am well aware of it, missing. As a result, it goes without saying that it wasn't a dialogue; or, if it must be one nevertheless, then a distorted [*faussé*], ruined dialogue (even though its remaining scraps were intact), without interlocutors or characters. Certainly not "me" and "me."

Nor you, surprising as that might seem.

This is borne out by the fact that it had nothing to do with the initial incident, with the *episode* that had in a way triggered the whole thing. And lest one misinterpret the term, one cannot reasonably say that it had some "dramatic" quality about it. No pain is dramatic. On the contrary, in my memory, in the memory that is left of it, this thing [*cela*], this muted ("silent") incantation, where I couldn't tell, however, who was deploring whom, kept unfurling itself, without end, pouring out in gusts, in slow, drawn-out gusts of rain dispersed by a violent wind, stirring heavy leaves, and which I didn't stop hearing that night. A sound, a huge rumbling: the ravage, the rage of the outside [*du dehors*].

. . . .

—No, it wasn't an image. Not in the least: decay [*déchéance*] (the outpouring [*épanchement*]) is without effigy.

That is why, come morning, in the mute light of what was indeed a white dawn, everything seemed washed by the rain that had not fallen, had not irrigated anything. No storm had taken place.

(As you know today, I could say it quite differently. In my deathly mythical style. So poignant is the pain of King Marke, of Golaud, it is sung. Declaimed. This song I know by heart; I could repeat this declamation. But pain, which touches worse than the heart, is dumbfounding [*interdit*].)

. . . .

—Having crossed the gravel surrounding the house (to the same sound of a storm that did not take place), I walked toward the end of the garden and stopped by the pile of earth and ash that you know, perhaps to look, beyond the fence, at the hazy hills—the plain. It wasn't yet winter, but it was cold, very cold. (It was the first time I'd stayed during that season in these parts, which are not mine any more than any other parts, and with which I'm not familiar, in spite of everything.) The animals had not yet stirred. Of course, nothing happened, but I knew that it had already happened to me: I knew it, without knowing it: I recognized the absolute novelty of it, the streaming [*ruissellement*], the weariness.

No, I wasn't speechless, but in a state of boundless indifference: I could die.

(Summer 1976–Summer 1981)

Notes

Translator's Note

1. Michael Syrotinski, "Fidelities," *Oxford Literary Review* 22, no. 1 (July 2000), special issue: "Disastrous Blanchot," 132–151; Philip Anderson, "The Contestation of Death," in *The Power of Contestation: Perspectives on Maurice Blanchot*, ed. Kevin Hart and Geoffrey Hartman (Baltimore, Md.: Johns Hopkins University Press, 2004), 141–155.

2. Alain Badiou, "'Dits' de Philippe Lacoue-Labarthe," *Lignes*, n.s., 22 (May 2007), special issue: "Philippe Lacoue-Labarthe," 19 (my translation).

3. Thomas Mann, "Freud and the Future," trans. H. T. Lowe-Porter, in *Essays of Three Decades* (London: Secker and Warburg, 1947), 411–428; Thomas Mann, "Freud und die Zufunkt" (1936), in *Gesammelte Werke in Dreizehn Bänden* (Frankfurt a. M.: Fischer, 1974), 9:478–501.

4. On *é-loignement*, see Philippe Lacoue-Labarthe, "Obliteration," trans. Thomas Trezise, in *The Subject of Philosophy*, ed. Thomas Trezise (Minneapolis: University of Minnesota Press, 1993), 62–72; Philippe Lacoue-Labarthe, "L'oblitération" (1973), in *Le sujet de la philosophie* (Paris: Aubier-Flammarion, 1979), 122–138; Philippe Lacoue-Labarthe, "Il faut," in *Heidegger and the Politics of Poetry*, trans. Jeff Fort (Urbana: University of Illinois Press, 2007), 38–59; Philippe Lacoue-Labarthe, "Il faut" (1992), in *Heidegger. La politique du poème* (Paris: Galilée, 2002), 79–115; and Philippe Lacoue-Labarthe, "In the Name of . . . ," in *Retreating the Political*, ed. and trans. Simon Sparks (London: Routledge, 1997), 55–78; Philippe Lacoue-Labarthe, "À Jacques Derrida—Au nom de . . ." (1980), in *L'imitation des modernes. Typographies II* (Paris: Galilée, 1986), 229–255.

5. See Lacoue-Labarthe, "Obliteration," 62–72; Lacoue-Labarthe, "L'oblitération," 122–138.

6. See Martin Heidegger, *Identité et différence* (1957), trans. André Préau, in *Questions I et II* (Paris: Gallimard, 1968), 298n1. For an English translation, see Martin Heidegger, *Identity and Difference*, trans. Joan Stambaugh (Chicago: University of Chicago Press, 1969), 64.

7. See Jacques Lacan, *Anxiety: The Seminar of Jacques Lacan, Book X*, ed. Jacques-Alain Miller, trans. A. R. Price (Cambridge: Polity, 2014), 12–13; Jacques Lacan, *Le séminaire, livre X. L'angoisse (1962–1963)*, ed. Jacques-Alain Miller (1982; Paris: Le Seuil, 2004), 21–23.

8. Philippe Lacoue-Labarthe, "The Echo of the Subject," trans. Barbara Harlow, in *Typography: Mimesis, Philosophy, Politics* (1989), ed. Christopher Fynsk (Stanford, Calif.: Stanford University Press, 1998), 189; Philippe Lacoue-Labarthe, "L'écho du sujet" (1975–1976), in *Le sujet de la philosophie*, 277.

9. See Philippe Lacoue-Labarthe, *Poetry as Experience*, trans. Andrea Tarnowski (Stanford, Calif.: Stanford University Press, 1999), 20; Philippe Lacoue-Labarthe, *La poésie comme expérience* (Paris: Bourgois, 1986), 33.

10. Antonin Artaud, notebook entry for April 14, 1946, *Cahiers de Rodez*, in *Œuvres complètes* (Paris: Gallimard, 1985), 26:64.

11. Lacoue-Labarthe, "The Echo of the Subject," 196; Lacoue-Labarthe, "L'écho du sujet," 285.

12. See Philippe Lacoue-Labarthe, "Typography," trans. Eduardo Cadava, in *Typography: Mimesis, Philosophy, Politics*, 43–138; Philippe Lacoue-Labarthe, "Typographie," in *Mimesis des articulations* (Paris: Flammarion, 1975), 165–270; and Philippe Lacoue-Labarthe, "La figure (humaine)" (1992), in *Écrits sur l'art*, posthumous ed. (Dijon: Les presses du réel, 2009), 189–199.

13. See Lacoue-Labarthe, "Il faut," 38–59; Lacoue-Labarthe, "Il faut," 79–115.

14. See Jacques Derrida, "Desistance," trans. Christopher Fynsk, in *Typography: Mimesis, Philosophy, Politics*, 1–42; Jacques Derrida, "Désistance" (1989), in *Psyché, Inventions de l'autre* (Paris: Galilée, 2003), 2:201–238.

15. Philippe Lacoue-Labarthe, "The Courage of Poetry," in *Heidegger and the Politics of Poetry*, 76; Philippe Lacoue-Labarthe, "Le courage de la poésie" (1993), in *Heidegger. La Politique du poème*, 146.

16. See Philippe Lacoue-Labarthe, "Phrase V (L'émoi)," in *Phrase* (Paris: Bourgois, 2000), 43.

Introduction
Aristide Bianchi and Leonid Kharlamov

1. Radio broadcast, "Tout arrive: spécial hommage à Maurice Blanchot," France Culture, February 25, 2003.

2. This brief draft for a "Post-scriptum" follows a parenthesis that can be found in the final text of Blanchot's essay collection *De Kafka à Kafka*, "The Very Last Word": "markers are still needed, however indecisive and however deceptive they may be" (Maurice Blanchot, *Friendship*, trans. Elizabeth Rottenberg [Stanford, Calif.: Stanford University Press, 1997], 279; Maurice Blanchot, *De Kafka à Kafka* [Paris: Gallimard, 1981], 238.) What the dates mentioned by Lacoue-Labarthe anticipate is relatively well known: following *Le 14 Juillet*, the "Declaration on the Right to Insubordination in the Algerian War" in 1960, and, from May 1968 to 1969, the Student-Writer Action Committee in the Service of the Movement, as well as the texts published in the review *Comité* and later in *Les Lettres Nouvelles* (all along with Dionys Mascolo).

3. "The Agony of Religion" (1997), in the present volume.

4. See Roger Laporte, *Une vie. Biographie* (Paris: POL, 1986); as well as the following texts by Lacoue-Labarthe devoted to Laporte: the back cover of Laporte's *Suite* (Paris: Hachette, 1979), the preface to his *Lettre à personne* (1989; Paris: Lignes, 2006), and the foreword to his *Carnet posthume* (Paris: Scheer, 2002).

5. See Philippe Lacoue-Labarthe and Jean-Luc Nancy, *The Literary Absolute: The Theory of Literature in German Romanticism*, trans. Philip Barnard and Cheryl Lester (New York: SUNY Press, 1988); Philippe Lacoue-Labarthe and Jean-Luc Nancy,

L'absolu littéraire: Théorie de la littérature du romantisme allemande (Paris: Le Seuil, 1978); as well as Mathieu Bénézet and Philippe Lacoue-Labarthe (including texts by Michel Deutsch, Emmanuel Hocquard, Roger Laporte, Jean-Luc Nancy, Jean-Louis Schefer, and Maurice Blanchot), *Misère de la littérature* (Paris: Bourgois, 1978).

6. See Philippe Lacoue-Labarthe and Jean-Luc Nancy, "The Nazi Myth," trans. Brian Holmes, *Critical Inquiry* 16, no. 2 (Winter 1990): 291–312 [this translation, to date the only existing English translation, is a translation of an earlier version of the text later published by L'Aube in 1991 (and subsequent editions) as *Le mythe nazi* (La Tour-d'Aigues: L'Aube, 2005)]; and Maurice Blanchot, "Intellectuals Under Scrutiny," trans. Michael Holland, in *The Blanchot Reader*, ed. Michael Holland (London: Blackwell, 1995), 206–227; Maurice Blanchot, *Les intellectuels en question* (1984; Tours: Farrago, 2000).

7. See *Gramma* 3–4 (1976), special issue: "Lire Blanchot, I"; *Gramma* 5 (1976), special issue: "Lire Blanchot, II."

8. Jeffrey Mehlman, *Legacies of Anti-Semitism in France* (Minneapolis: University of Minnesota Press, 1983).

9. Philippe Lacoue-Labarthe, letter to Maurice Blanchot, July 6, 1984, unpublished.

10. See Jean-Luc Nancy, *Maurice Blanchot. Passion politique* (Paris: Galilée, 2011). One can infer Lacoue-Labarthe's position from Dionys Mascolo's letter (collected in the work just cited), which is both a response to and rejection of this position.

11. Radio broadcast, "Tout arrive: spécial hommage à Maurice Blanchot."

12. See Jean-Luc Nancy, *Maurice Blanchot. Passion politique*, 47–62.

13. While the said work on Heidegger had been initiated within the framework of the Center of Philosophical Research on the Political, which Lacoue-Labarthe and Nancy founded in late 1980 at the ENS in Paris (cf. Philippe Lacoue-Labarthe, "Transcendence Ends in Politics," trans. Peter Caws, in *Typography: Mimesis, Philosophy, Politics*, ed. Christopher Fynsk [1989; Stanford, Calif.: Stanford University Press, 1998], 267–300; Philippe Lacoue-Labarthe, "La transcendance finit/e dans le politique" (1981), in *L'imitation des modernes* [Paris: Galilée, 1986], 135–173), the bulk of this work was carried out in Philippe Lacoue-Labarthe, *Heidegger, Art, and Politics: The Fiction of the Political* (trans. Chris Turner [Oxford: Blackwell, 1990]; Philippe Lacoue-Labarthe, *La fiction du politique* [Paris: Bourgois, 1987]), that is, between the abandoned number of the *Cahiers de l'Herne* and the resumption of the project exclusively around the political question. This work would also be the subject of an exchange with Blanchot or at least clearly drew the latter's attention. It was in fact at Blanchot's instigation that extracts from *The Fiction of the Political* would be published (preceded by a letter in which Blanchot noted the importance of Lacoue-Labarthe's book) in an issue put together by Catherine David for *Le Nouvel Observateur* that appeared on 22 January 1988 (see Maurice Blanchot, "[Thinking the Apocalypse]," in *Political Writings, 1953–1993*, ed. and trans. Zakir Paul [New York: Fordham University Press, 2010], 119–123; Maurice Blanchot, "[Penser l'apocalypse]" (1988), in *Écrits politiques. Guerre d'Algérie, Mai 68, etc. (1958–1993)*, ed. Michel Surya [Paris: Lignes/Scheer, 2003], 155–163).

14. Lacoue-Labarthe recounts this in more detail in "Fidelities" (1997), in the present volume.

15. See "Dismay" (1978; 2000), in the present volume.

16. "The previous one" refers here to "Phrase I," first published by Emmanuel Hocquard in a collection entitled *Chutes* (Paris: Orange Export Ltd., 1977) and reprinted in Philippe Lacoue-Labarthe, *Phrase* (Paris: Bourgois, 2000), 9–10.

17. See Maurice Blanchot, *The Writing of the Disaster*, trans. Ann Smock (Lincoln: University of Nebraska Press, 1995), 114–116, 137–138; Maurice Blanchot, *L'écriture du désastre* (Paris: Gallimard, 1980), 176–179, 207–208.

18. Philippe Lacoue-Labarthe, "[En 1976, Maurice Blanchot . . .]," unspecified conference paper, 1998–2002 (?), unpublished.

19. Philippe Lacoue-Labarthe and Jean-Luc Nancy, "*Noli me frangere*," trans. Brian Holmes, in Jean-Luc Nancy, *The Birth to Presence*, trans. Brian Holmes et al. (Stanford, Calif.: Stanford University Press, 1993), 266–278; Philippe Lacoue-Labarthe and Jean-Luc Nancy, "*Noli me frangere*" (1982), *Europe* 973 (May 2010), special issue: "Philippe Lacoue-Labarthe," 32–42.

20. "The fragment, as fragments, tends to dissolve the totality which it presupposes and which it carries off toward the dissolution from which it does not (strictly speaking) form, but to which it exposes itself so that, disappearing—and along with it, all identity—it maintains itself as the energy of disappearing"; Maurice Blanchot, *The Writing of the Disaster*, 60; *L'écriture du désastre*, 99–100. Blanchot's italics.

21. Lacoue-Labarthe and Nancy, "*Noli me frangere*," 270–271; Lacoue-Labarthe and Nancy, "*Noli me frangere*," 36.

22. Lacoue-Labarthe and Nancy, "*Noli me frangere*," 277–278; Lacoue-Labarthe and Nancy, "*Noli me frangere*," 42.

23. Georges Bataille, *Manet*, trans. Austryn Wainhouse and James Emmons (London: MacMillan, 1983), 48; Georges Bataille, *Manet* (1955), in *Œuvres complètes* (Paris: Gallimard, 1979), 9:133.

24. On the crypteia, see Plato, *Laws* I.633b; Plutarch, *Lycurgus* 28; Henri Jeanmaire, "La cryptie lacédémonienne," *Revue des études grecques* 26 (1913): 121–150; Pierre Vidal-Naquet, *The Black Hunter*, trans. Andrew Szegedy-Maszak (Baltimore, Md.: Johns Hopkins University Press, 1986); Pierre Vidal-Naquet, *Le chasseur noir* (Paris: Maspero, 1981).

25. See Jacques Derrida, *Demeure: Fiction and Testimony*, trans. Elizabeth Rottenberg (Stanford, Calif.: Stanford University Press, 2000); Jacques Derrida, *Demeure. Maurice Blanchot* (Paris: Galilée, 1998).

26. Actually, nine years (September 22, 1994–October 13, 2003).

27. See Christophe Bident, *Maurice Blanchot. Partenaire invisible* (Seyssel: Champ Vallon, 1998), esp. 228–232, 581–583.

28. Maurice Blanchot, "Kafka and the Work's Demand," in *The Space of Literature*, trans. Ann Smock (Lincoln: University of Nebraska Press, 1982), 59; Maurice Blanchot, "Kafka et l'exigence de l'œuvre" (1952), in *De Kafka à Kafka*, 96.

29. Maurice Blanchot, letter to Jacques Derrida, July 20, 1994, quoted in Derrida, *Demeure: Fiction and Testimony*, 83; Derrida, *Demeure. Maurice Blanchot*, 64.

30. Presumably, 1958 is the date Lacoue-Labarthe is assigning here to the publication of Blanchot's "Kafka and the Work's Demand." In point of fact, the article first appeared in March 1952 in *Critique* 58 before being collected in 1955 in *The Space of Literature* and again in 1986 in *De Kafka à Kafka*.

31. Maurice Blanchot, *The Infinite Conversation*, trans. Susan Hanson (Minneapolis:

University of Minnesota Press, 1993), 114–115; Maurice Blanchot, *L'entretien infini* (Paris: Gallimard, 1969), 166.

32. Blanchot, "Intellectuals Under Scrutiny," 221; Blanchot, *Les intellectuels en question*, 48.

33. Like those that follow, this extract was transcribed from a recording of Lacoue-Labarthe's paper "Fidelities," given at the Cerisy-la-Salle conference entitled "L'animal autobiographique, autour du travail de Jacques Derrida," which took place on July 14, 1997. We would like to thank in particular Makoto Asari for having donated these recordings (as well as many others) to the archives.

34. Lacoue-Labarthe and Nancy, *Le mythe nazi*, 74. [As the annex in question was added in 1992 to an augmented edition of Lacoue-Labarthe's and Nancy's text, it does not appear in Brian Holmes's translation (published in 1990), which is based on an earlier version of the text.]

35. Lacoue-Labarthe and Nancy, "The Nazi Myth," 307; Lacoue-Labarthe and Nancy, *Le mythe nazi*, 57–58.

36. See Philippe Lacoue-Labarthe and Jean-Luc Nancy, "Mythes et croyances," conference paper delivered at Schiltigheim on May 7, 1980, and published in the conference proceedings entitled "Les mécanismes du fascisme," Colmar, Bibliothèque centrale de prêt du Haut-Rhin, 1981.

37. Philippe Lacoue-Labarthe and Jean-Luc Nancy, "The Jewish People Do Not Dream," part 2, trans. Brian Holmes, *Stanford Literature Review* 8, no. 1–2 (Spring/Fall 1991): 50; Philippe Lacoue-Labarthe and Jean-Luc Nancy, "Le peuple juif ne rêve pas," in *La psychanalyse est-elle une histoire juive?*, ed. Adélie Rassial and Jean-Jacques Rassial (Paris: Le Seuil, 1981), 87; reprinted in *La panique politique* (Paris: Bourgois, 2013), 98–99.

38. See "[In 1976, Malraux . . .]" (1997), in the present volume.

39. "[In 1976, Malraux . . .]", in the present volume. Lacoue-Labarthe's italics.

40. "[In 1976, Malraux . . .]", in the present volume.

41. "[In 1976, Malraux . . .]", in the present volume. Lacoue-Labarthe's italics.

42. Thomas Mann, "Freud and the Future," trans. H.T. Lowe-Porter, in *Essays of Three Decades* (London: Secker and Warburg, 1947), 425; Thomas Mann, "Freud und die Zufunkt" (1936), in *Gesammelte Werke in Dreizehn Bänden* (Frankfurt a. M.: Fischer, 1974), 9:497.

43. See Maurice Blanchot, *Faux pas*, trans. Charlotte Mandell (Stanford, Calif.: Stanford University Press, 2001), 31; Maurice Blanchot, *Faux pas* (Paris: Gallimard, 1943), 40.

44. "With full knowledge of the facts": the phrase punctuates, a few months after "Dismay," a text entitled "Précis," which Lacoue-Labarthe devoted to Mathieu Bénézet, the writer. In this text, worklessness [*désœuvrement*] is tied to the motif of an impossible exit [*sortie*] from citation: "literature, or, more exactly, that which defines *itself* as literature, is the *recitation of a subject*. [. . .] To write, 'to go in for writing,' is—and has always been—to set out to win out over citation [*regagner sur la citation*], or, if one prefers, to cite myth itself, as itself, in its own element (language), or even: to create myth (the Greeks called this *mythopoiesis*)—in short, to *re-cite* myth. [. . .] And in truth, one never comes back from mimetism (one never wins out over citation, one is always *written*), for there is no *knowledge* of mimetism. Nor any consciousness of it, as one can well imagine. [. . .] There is only repetition, under that which seeks, each time, to be born, to *orga-*

nize itself as literature, to constitute itself as *work*, out of the same breakdown, the same dislocation, the same termination [*avortement*]. Literature 'is' this infinite, hardly audible murmur of *worklessness*. Which is to say, also, this infinite, hardly perceptible disorganization of the subject." Philippe Lacoue-Labarthe, "Précis," *Critique* 357 (February 1977): 147–149; Lacoue-Labarthe's italics.

45. Philippe Lacoue-Labarthe, "L'instance de la mort," seminar series conducted within the framework of the Paris Program in Critical Theory, organized by Samuel Weber at Northwestern University (Chicago), Paris, Spring 2005.

46. See "Ending and Unending Agony" (2003), in the present volume, where Lacoue-Labarthe specifies the need to return to this question.

47. See Maurice Blanchot, "Discours sur la patience," *Le Nouveau Commerce* 30–31 (Spring 1975): 19–44.

48. Like those that follow, this "quotation" was pieced together on the basis of notes (our own) taken by listeners in the audience: speaking from his own succinct notes, Lacoue-Labarthe thus never actually *wrote* these sentences.

49. Blanchot, *The Writing of the Disaster*, 114; Blanchot, *L'écriture du désastre*, 177.

50. See Philippe Lacoue-Labarthe, *Préface à "La disparition,"* ed. Jean-Christophe Bailly (Paris: Bourgois, 2009). The extracts by Blanchot used as epigraphs to "La disparition" are drawn from *The Instant of My Death* and *The Writing of the Disaster.*

51. Lacoue-Labarthe, *Préface à "La disparition,"* 45–46. Lacoue-Labarthe's italics.

Prologue

1. Jorge Luis Borges, "The Secret Miracle," in *Fictions*, trans. Andrew Hurley (London: Penguin, 2000), 124; Jorge Luis Borges, "El milagro secreto" (1943), in *Ficciones, Obras completas* (Buenos Aires: Emecé, 1966), 5:159.

2. Readers familiar with Blanchot's work will have recognized in Lacoue-Labarthe's quotation marks and italics the eponymous titles of Blanchot's postwar narratives: *Death Sentence* [*L'arrêt de mort*] (1948), *When the Time Comes* [*Au moment voulu*] (1951), and *The Instant of My Death* [*L'instant de ma mort*] (1994).

3. See Sigmund Freud, "Analysis Terminable and Interminable," in *The Standard Edition of the Complete Psychological Works of Sigmund Freud*, ed. James Strachey (London: Vintage, 2001), 23:211–253; Sigmund Freud, "Die endliche und die unendliche Analyse" (1937), in *Gesammelte Werke* (Frankfurt a. M.: Fischer, 1991), 16:57–99. The first French translation of this essay, by Anne Berman, was entitled "Analyse terminée, analyse interminable," *Revue française de psychanalyse* 9, no. 1 (1939): 3–38; Berman's translation was republished under the same title in 1975, *Revue française de psychanalyse* 39, no. 3 (May–June 1975): 371–402.

4. See Blanchot's essay on Paul Celan, "The Last to Speak," which first appeared in the *Revue de Belles-Lettres* (March 1972) before being reprinted as a book (1984; 1986) and subsequently collected in *A Voice from Elsewhere*, trans. Charlotte Mandell (Albany, N.Y.: SUNY Press, 2007), 53–93; Maurice Blanchot, *Une voix venue d'ailleurs* (Paris: Gallimard, 2002), 69–107.

5. Paul Celan, "The Meridian," in *Selected Poems and Prose of Paul Celan*, trans. John Felstiner (New York: Norton, 2001), 408; Paul Celan, "Der Meridian" (1960),

in *Gesammelte Werke in fünf Bänden* (Frankfurt a. M.: Suhrkamp, 1983), 3:196. See also Philippe Lacoue-Labarthe, "Remembering Dates," in *Poetry as Experience*, trans. Andrea Tarnowski (Stanford, Calif.: Stanford University Press, 1999), 39–123; Philippe Lacoue-Labarthe, "La mémoire des dates," in *La poésie comme expérience* (Paris: Bourgois, 1986), 59–168.

Fidelities

1. On Blanchot's notion of "ressassement éternel" (the phrase also served as the title of a 1951 volume by Blanchot collecting two short narratives first published separately in journals in 1947; a third publication of these narratives, augmented with an afterword, subsequently appeared in 1983 under the title *Vicious Circles* [*Après coup*]), see Maurice Blanchot, *The Space of Literature*, trans. Ann Smock (Lincoln: University of Nebraska Press, 1982), 238, 246; Maurice Blanchot, *L'espace littéraire* (1955; Paris: Gallimard, 1988), 319, 331. See also Philippe Lacoue-Labarthe, "The Fable (Literature and Philosophy)," in *The Subject of Philosophy*, ed. Thomas Trezise (Minneapolis: University of Minnesota Press, 1993), 9, 13; Philippe Lacoue-Labarthe, "La fable (Littérature et philosophie)" (1970), in *Le sujet de la philosophie. Typographies I* (Paris: Aubier-Flammarion, 1979), 22, 28.

2. See Jacques Derrida, *Demeure: Fiction and Testimony*, trans. Elizabeth Rottenberg (Stanford, Calif.: Stanford University Press, 1998); Jacques Derrida, *Demeure: Maurice Blanchot* (Paris: Editions Galilée, 1998).

3. Lacoue-Labarthe is referring to the parentheses and question mark that accompany the title: "(A Primal Scene?)." See Maurice Blanchot, *The Writing of the Disaster*, trans. Ann Smock (Lincoln: University of Nebraska Press, 1995), 72; Maurice Blanchot, *L'écriture du désastre* (Paris: Gallimard, 1980), 117. See also the title essay of the present volume, "Ending and Unending Agony," as well as the "Interview with Pascal Possoz."

4. Blanchot, *The Writing of the Disaster*, 72; Blanchot, *L'écriture du désastre*, 117.

5. Immanuel Kant, *Critique of Pure Reason*, ed. and trans. Paul Guyer and Allen W. Wood (Cambridge: Cambridge University Press, 1998), 273; Immanuel Kant, *Kritik der reinen Vernunft* (1781; 1787), in *Werke in zehn Bänden*, ed. Wilhelm Weischedel (Darmstadt: Wissenschaftliche Buchgesellschaft, 1975), 190.

6. Friedrich Hölderlin, "Remarks on *Antigone*," in *Essays and Letters on Theory*, trans. Thomas Pfau (Albany, N.Y.: SUNY Press, 1988), 113; Friedrich Hölderlin, "Anmerkungen zur *Antigonae*" (1804), in *Antigone de Sophocle*, bilingual ed., trans. Philippe Lacoue-Labarthe (Paris: Bourgois, 1998), 168.

7. G. W. F. Hegel, *Natural Law*, trans. T. M. Knox (Philadelphia: University of Pennsylvania Press, 1975), 104; G. W. F. Hegel, *Über die wissenschaftlichen Behandlungsarten des Naturrechts* (1802–1803), in *Werke in zwanzig Bänden* (Frankfurt a. M.: Suhrkamp, 1970), 2:495.

8. G. W. F. Hegel, *Phenomenology of Spirit*, trans. A. V. Miller (Oxford: Oxford University Press, 1977), 455; G. W. F. Hegel, *Phänomenologie des Geistes* (1807), in *Werke in zwanzig Bänden* (Frankfurt a. M.: Suhrkamp, 1970), 3:547.

9. Georges Bataille, "Hegel, Death, and Sacrifice," trans. Jonathan Strauss, *Yale French*

Studies 78 (1990): 10; Georges Bataille, "Hegel, la mort et le sacrifice" (1955), in *Œuvres complètes* (Paris: Gallimard, 1988), 12:327.

10. Bataille, "Hegel, Death, and Sacrifice," 13; Bataille, "Hegel, la mort et le sacrifice," 12:329–330.

11. Bataille, "Hegel, Death, and Sacrifice," 14; Bataille, "Hegel, la mort et le sacrifice," 12:331.

12. Blanchot, *The Writing of the Disaster*, 67; Blanchot, *L'écriture du désastre*, 110.

13. Bataille, "Hegel, Death, and Sacrifice," 18; Bataille, "Hegel, la mort et le sacrifice," 12:335.

14. See "Birth Is Death" (1994), in the present volume.

15. Friedrich Hölderlin, "In lovely blueness . . . ," in *Poems and Fragments*, bilingual ed., trans. Michael Hamburger (London: Anvil Press Poetry, 2004), 793; Friedrich Hölderlin, "In lieblicher Bläue . . ." (1823), ibid., 792.

16. The French philosopher Sarah Kofman (1934–1994).

17. The French philosopher Jean-Luc Nancy (b. 1940).

18. The opening lines of the *Iliad*: "Sing, goddess, of the wrath"—"μῆνιν ἄειδε θεὰ."

19. Thomas Mann, "Freud and the Future," trans. H. T. Lowe-Porter, in *Essays of Three Decades* (London: Secker and Warburg, 1947), 425; Thomas Mann, "Freud und die Zufunkt" (1936), in *Gesammelte Werke in Dreizehn Bänden* (Frankfurt a. M.: Fischer, 1974), 9:497.

20. Maurice Blanchot, *The Instant of My Death*, trans. Elizabeth Rottenberg (Stanford, Calif.: Stanford University Press, 2000), 3; Maurice Blanchot, *L'instant de ma mort* (1994; Paris: Gallimard, 2002), 10.

21. Blanchot, *The Instant of My Death*, 7; Blanchot, *L'instant de ma mort*, 13–14.

22. Blanchot, *The Instant of My Death*, 3, 5; Blanchot, *L'instant de ma mort*, 10, 11.

23. Blanchot, *The Instant of My Death*, 5; Blanchot, *L'instant de ma mort*, 11.

24. Blanchot, *The Instant of My Death*, 5; Blanchot, *L'instant de ma mort*, 11–12.

25. The sentence is quoted in Louis Racine's "Discours préliminaire des remarques sur les tragédies de Jean Racine," in Racine, *Œuvres complètes* (Geneva: Slatkine, 1969), 5:271, a facsimile of the 1808 Le Normant edition (my translation).

26. Blanchot, *The Writing of the Disaster*, 36; Blanchot, *L'écriture du désastre*, 61.

27. Blanchot, *The Writing of the Disaster*, 65; Blanchot, *L'écriture du désastre*, 108.

28. See Jacques Derrida, "Introduction: Desistance," trans. Christopher Fynsk, in *Typography: Mimesis, Philosophy, Politics*, ed. Christopher Fynsk (Stanford, Calif.: Stanford University Press, 1998), 1–42; Jacques Derrida, "Désistance" (1989), in *Psyché, Inventions de l'autre* (Paris: Galilée, 2003), 2:201–238.

29. See Jean-Luc Nancy, *Maurice Blanchot. Passion politique* (Paris: Galilée, 2011), 47–62.

30. The *Nouvelle Revue Française*.

31. Blanchot, *The Instant of My Death*, 11; Blanchot, *L'instant de ma mort*, 18.

32. André Malraux, *The Walnut Trees of Altenburg*, trans. A. W. Fielding (Chicago: University of Chicago Press, 1992), 227; André Malraux, *Les noyers de l'Altenburg* (1943; 1948), in *Œuvres complètes* (Paris: Gallimard, 1996), 2:765. Here, as below, Lacoue-Labarthe is quoting from the earlier version of Malraux's text (*Les noyers de l'Altenburg*) and not from the version later collected in the *Antimémoires*.

33. Blanchot, *The Writing of the Disaster*, 72; Blanchot, *L'écriture du désastre*, 117.

34. Lacoue-Labarthe is referring to his defense of his *doctorat d'État* (Derrida was a member of the examining committee), which formed the basis for *Heidegger, Art, and Politics: The Fiction of the Political*, trans. Chris Turner (Oxford: Blackwell, 1990); *La fiction du politique: Heidegger, l'art et la politique* (Paris: Bourgois, 1987).

The Contestation of Death

1. See Lacoue-Labarthe's "Note," appended to the end of this text.

2. See "Birth Is Death," in the present volume.

3. Friedrich Nietzsche, *Ecce Homo*, in *The Anti-Christ, Ecce Homo, Twilight of the Idols and Other Writings*, ed. Aaron Ridley, trans. Judith Norman (Cambridge: Cambridge University Press, 2005), 74–75; Friedrich Nietzsche, *Ecce Homo* (1889), in *Werke: Kritische Gesamtausgabe*, vol. 4, part 3 (Berlin: de Gruyter, 1969), 262.

4. Stéphane Mallarmé to Henri Cazalis, May 14, 1867, in *Selected Letters of Stéphane Mallarmé*, trans. Rosemary Lloyd (Chicago: University of Chicago Press, 1988), 74; Stéphane Mallarmé, *Correspondance complète, 1862–1871* (Paris: Gallimard, 1995), 342.

5. Mallarmé to Eugène Lefébure, May 27, 1867, in *Selected Letters of Stéphane Mallarmé*, 77; Mallarmé, *Correspondance complète*, 389.

6. Edgar Allan Poe, "The Facts in the Case of M. Valdemar" (1845), in *The Fall of the House of Usher and Other Writings*, ed. David Galloway (London: Penguin, 1986), 359. The original English actually reads: "*I say to you that I am dead!*" which Baudelaire translates as: "*Je vous dis que je suis mort!*" The nobiliary particle ("Monsieur *de* Valdemar") is absent from the original.

7. Jean-Jacques Rousseau, *Reveries of the Solitary Walker*, trans. Russell Goulbourne (Oxford: Oxford University Press, 2011), 56; Jean-Jacques Rousseau, *Les rêveries du promeneur solitaire* (1782), in *Œuvres complètes* (Paris: Gallimard, 1959), 1:1047.

8. Michel de Montaigne, "On Practice," in *Essays*, trans. M. A. Screech (London: Penguin, 2003), book 2, 417; Michel de Montaigne, "De l'exercitation," in *Les essais*, ed. Pierre Villey (Paris: PUF, 1988), book 2, 371.

9. Montaigne, "On Practice," 424; Montaigne, "De l'exercitation," 377.

10. Martin Heidegger, *Off the Beaten Track*, ed. and trans. Julian Young and Kenneth Haynes (Cambridge: Cambridge University Press, 2002), 182; Martin Heidegger, *Holzwege* (1950; Frankfurt a. M.: Klostermann, 2003), 244.

11. See also Philippe Lacoue-Labarthe, *Poetry as Experience*, trans. Andrea Tarnowski (Stanford, Calif.: Stanford University Press, 1999), 128n15; Philippe Lacoue-Labarthe, *La poésie comme expérience* (Paris: Bourgois, 1986), 30–31n6.

12. See Plato, *The Republic*, trans. Robin Waterfield (Oxford: Oxford University Press, 2008), 394c, 89–90.

13. See Jean-Luc Nancy, *Maurice Blanchot. Passion politique* (Paris: Galilée, 2011), 47–62.

14. Paul Celan, "Ash-aureole," in *Selected Poems and Prose of Paul Celan*, trans. John Felstiner (New York: Norton, 2001), 261; Paul Celan, "Aschenglorie . . ." (1964), in *Atemwende*, in *Werke: Historische-kritische Ausgabe*, vol. 7, part 1 (Frankfurt a. M.: Suhrkamp, 1990), 72.

15. Maurice Blanchot, *The Instant of My Death*, trans. Elizabeth Rottenberg (Stanford, Calif.: Stanford University Press, 2000), 5; Maurice Blanchot, *L'instant de ma mort*, (1994; Paris: Gallimard, 2002), 11.

16. Maurice Blanchot, *The Writing of the Disaster*, trans. Ann Smock (Lincoln: University of Nebraska Press, 1995), 72; Maurice Blanchot, *L'écriture du désastre* (Paris: Gallimard, 1980), 117.

17. See also Philippe Lacoue-Labarthe, "The Echo of the Subject," trans. Barbara Harlow, in *Typography: Mimesis, Philosophy, Politics*, ed. Christopher Fynsk (Stanford, Calif.: Stanford University Press, 1998), 139–207, esp. 179–180); Philippe Lacoue-Labarthe, "L'écho du sujet" (1975–1976), in *Le sujet de la philosophie. Typographies I* (Paris: Aubier-Flammarion, 1979), 217–303, esp. 265–266.

18. Stéphane Mallarmé, "Arthur Rimbaud," in *Divagations*, trans. Barbara Johnson (Cambridge, Mass.: Harvard University Press, 2007), 69; Stéphane Mallarmé, "Arthur Rimbaud" (1896), in *Divagations*, in *Œuvres complètes* (Paris: Gallimard, 2003), 2:125.

19. See Jacques Derrida, "Introduction: Desistance," trans. Christopher Fynsk, in *Typography: Mimesis, Philosophy, Politics*, ed. Christopher Fynsk (Stanford, Calif.: Stanford University Press, 1998), 1–42; Jacques Derrida, "Désistance" (1989), in *Psyché, Inventions de l'autre* (Paris: Galilée, 2003), 2:201–238.

20. Plato, *Phaedo*, trans. David Gallop (Oxford: Oxford University Press, 2009), 81a, 32.

21. Montaigne, "On Practice," 418; Montaigne, "De l'exercitation," 373.

22. Montaigne, "On Practice," 418; Montaigne, "De l'exercitation," 373.

23. Montaigne, "On Practice," 425; Montaigne, "De l'exercitation," 379.

24. Montaigne, "On Practice," 420; Montaigne, "De l'exercitation," 374.

25. Montaigne, "On Practice," 418; Montaigne, "De l'exercitation," 373.

26. Blanchot, *The Instant of My Death*, 3; Blanchot, *L'instant de ma mort*, 10.

27. In truth, Blanchot seems to have first met Bataille as early as late 1940. See Maurice Blanchot, "Intellectuals Under Scrutiny," in *The Blanchot Reader*, ed. and trans. Michael Holland (Oxford: Blackwell, 1995), 226n8; Blanchot, *Les intellectuels en question* (1984; Tours: Farrago, 2000), 41n7; and Georges Bataille, "Notice autobiographique" (1958 [?]), in *Œuvres complètes* (Paris: Gallimard, 1976), 7:462.

28. Friedrich Nietzsche, *Nachgelassene Fragmente 1869–1874*, in *Sämtliche Werke: Kritische Studienausgabe in 15 Bänden* (Munich: Deutscher Taschenbuch, 1999), 7:42 (my translation). Together with other fragments and notes dating from the period 1869–1872, Lacoue-Labarthe translated this note in Friedrich Nietzsche, *La naissance de la tragédie. Fragments posthumes: automne 1869– printemps 1972*, in Friedrich Nietzsche, *Œuvres philosophiques complètes*, vol. 1, part 1 (Paris: Gallimard, 1977), 184. See also Philippe Lacoue-Labarthe, "Apocryphal Nietzsche," trans. Timothy D. Bent, in *The Subject of Philosophy*, ed. Thomas Trezise (Minneapolis: University of Minnesota Press, 1993), 51; Philippe Lacoue-Labarthe, "Nietzsche Apocryphe" (1973), in *Le sujet de la philosophie*, 100.

29. Plato, *Phaedo*, 59b, 3. Phaedo's exact words are: "Plato, I believe, was unwell"—"Πλάτων δὲ οἶμαι ἠσθένει."

30. Socrates actually appears in four "fragments" (or "fragmentaries") of *The Writing of the Disaster*, 35, 62–63, 65, 74; Blanchot, *L'écriture du désastre*, 60, 103, 107, 119.

31. Maurice Blanchot to Roger Laporte, April 13, 1987, Philippe Lacoue-Labarthe Archives, Institut Mémoires de l'édition contemporaine (IMEC), unpublished.

1. Birth Is Death

1. The French philosopher Sarah Kofman (1934–1994).

2. Friedrich Hölderlin, "In lovely blueness . . . ," in *Poems and Fragments*, bilingual ed., trans. Michael Hamburger (London: Anvil Press Poetry, 2004), 793; Friedrich Hölderlin, "In lieblicher Bläue . . ." (1823), ibid., 792.

3. Friedrich Hölderlin, "Patmos," in *Poems and Fragments*, bilingual ed., trans. Michael Hamburger (London: Anvil Press Poetry, 2004), 551; Friedrich Hölderlin, "Patmos" (1823), ibid., 550.

4. Friedrich Hölderlin, letter to his brother, January 1, 1799, in *Essays and Letters on Theory*, trans. Thomas Pfau (Albany, N.Y.: SUNY Press, 1988), 137; Friedrich Hölderlin, *Sämtliche Werke und Briefe* (Frankfurt a. M.: Deutscher Klassiker, 1992), 3:331.

5. Lacoue-Labarthe is referring to Blanchot's work *The Step Not Beyond*, published in 1973. For a discussion of Blanchot's notion of the step (not) beyond (*pas au-delà*), see Philippe Lacoue-Labarthe, "Le règne," *Nouvelle Barre du Jour* 216–217 (1989), special issue: "La mort du genre 2," 83–107.

6. Stéphane Mallarmé, "Verlaine's Tomb," in *Sonnets*, trans. David Scott (Exeter: Shearsman, 2008), 93; Stéphane Mallarmé, "Tombeau" (1897), in *Œuvres complètes* (Paris: Gallimard, 1998), 1:39.

7. Stéphane Mallarmé, letter to Eugène Lefébure, May 27, 1867, in *Selected Letters of Stéphane Mallarmé*, trans. Rosemary Lloyd (Chicago: University of Chicago Press, 1988), 77; Stéphane Mallarmé, *Correspondance complète, 1862–1871* (Paris: Gallimard, 1995), 389.

8. Stéphane Mallarmé, letter to Henri Cazalis, May 14, 1867, in *Selected Letters of Stéphane Mallarmé*, 74; Stéphane Mallarmé, *Correspondance complète, 1862–1871*, 342.

2. The Agony of Religion

1. Walter Benjamin, "On the Concept of History," in *Selected Writings*, trans. Edmund Jephcott et al., ed. Howard Eiland and Michael W. Jennings (Cambridge, Mass.: Harvard University Press, 2003), 4:392; Walter Benjamin, "Über den Begriff der Geschichte" (1940), in *Gesammelte Schriften*, vol. 1, part 2 (Frankfurt a. M.: Suhrkamp, 1974), 696.

2. See "Birth Is Death," in the present volume.

3. Maurice Blanchot, *The Writing of the Disaster*, trans. Ann Smock (Lincoln: University of Nebraska Press, 1995), 72; Maurice Blanchot, *L'écriture du désastre* (Paris: Gallimard, 1980), 117.

Ending and Unending Agony

1. Jean-Jacques Rousseau, *The Confessions*, trans. J. M. Cohen (London: Penguin, 1953), 218; Jean-Jacques Rousseau, *Les confessions* (1782–1789), in *Œuvres complètes* (Paris: Gallimard, 1959), 1:228.

2. Lacoue-Labarthe's substantival reference to Blanchot's "fragmentaries" [*fragmentaires*] reflects Blanchot's own distinction—in conceptual terms but also as a practice or genre of writing—between what he calls "the fragmentary" [*le fragmentaire*] and the fragment [*le fragment*]. The notion of the fragmentary figures prominently in Blanchot's *The Writing of the Disaster* but also in earlier work, from *Awaiting Oblivion* (1962) onward.

3. See Sigmund Freud, "On Narcissism: An Introduction," in *The Standard Edition of the Complete Psychological Works of Sigmund Freud*, trans. James Strachey (London: Hogarth Press, 1957), 14:73–102; Sigmund Freud, "Zur Einführung des Narzissmuss" (1914), in *Gesammelte Werke* (Frankfurt a. M.: Fischer, 1981), 10:137–170. On the notion of the "primal scene," see also Freud's "From the History of an Infantile Neurosis," in *The Standard Edition of the Complete Psychological Works of Sigmund Freud*, trans. James Strachey (London: Hogarth Press, 1955), 17:7–122; Sigmund Freud, "Aus der Geschichte einer infantilen Neurose" (1918), in *Gesammelte Werke* (Frankfurt a. M.: Fischer, 2006), 12:27–157.

4. In addition to having been an influential editor (*Empreintes*, *Digraphe*, *Première Livraison*), Mathieu Bénézet (1946–2013) was also the author of numerous books, including *L'histoire de la peinture en trois volumes* (Paris: Gallimard, 1968), *L'aphonie de Hegel, poésie* (Sens: Obsidiane, 2000), and *Et nous n'apprîmes rien: poésie (1962–1979)* (Paris: Flammarion, 2002), as well as an essay on Blanchot entitled "M. B. par M. B.," collected in *Maurice Blanchot. Récits critiques*, ed. Christophe Bident and Pierre Vilar (Tours/Paris: Lignes/Scheer, 2003), 435–438.

5. See Blaise Pascal, "The Memorial," in *Pensées and Other Writings*, trans. Honor Levi (Oxford: Oxford University Press, 1995), 178; Blaise Pascal, "Fragment 711 (Mémorial)" (1670), in *Œuvres complètes* (Paris: Gallimard, 2000), 2:851–852.

6. See Jacques Lacan, *The Ethics of Psychoanalysis, 1959–1960: The Seminar of Jacques Lacan, Book VII*, ed. Jacques-Alain Miller, trans. Dennis Porter (London: Routledge, 2008); Jacques Lacan, *Le séminaire, livre VII. L'éthique de la psychanalyse: 1959–1960*, ed. Jacques-Alain Miller (Paris: Le Seuil, 1986).

7. Donald Winnicott, "Fear of Breakdown" (1974), in *Psycho-Analytic Explorations*, ed. Clare Winnicott, Ray Shepherd, and Madeleine Davis (London: Karnac, 1989), 90, 91.

8. Serge Leclaire, *A Child Is Being Killed: On Primary Narcissism and the Death Drive*, trans. Marie-Claude Hays (Stanford, Calif.: Stanford University Press, 1998), 4; Serge Leclaire, *On tue un enfant: un essai sur le narcissisme primaire et la pulsion de mort* (1975) (Paris: Le Seuil, 1981), 13.

9. See "Fidelities" and "The Contestation of Death," in the present volume.

10. See Georges Bataille, *Inner Experience*, trans. Leslie Boldt (Albany, N.Y.: SUNY Press, 1988), 7, 12, 53, 102; Georges Bataille, *L'expérience intérieure* (1941), in *Œuvres complètes* (Paris: Gallimard, 1973), 5:19, 24, 67, 120.

11. See Philippe Lacoue-Labarthe, "The Caesura of the Speculative," trans. Robert Eisenhauer, in *Typography: Mimesis, Philosophy, Politics*, ed. Christopher Fynsk (Stanford, Calif.: Stanford University Press, 1998), 208–235; Philippe Lacoue-Labarthe, "La césure du spéculatif" (1978), in *L'imitation des modernes* (Paris: Galilée, 1986), 39–69.

12. Maurice Blanchot, *The Instant of My Death*, trans. Elizabeth Rottenberg (Stan-

ford, Calif.: Stanford University Press, 2000), 5, 7; Maurice Blanchot, *L'instant de ma mort* (1994; Paris: Gallimard, 2002), 11.

13. See Maurice Blanchot, *The Infinite Conversation*, trans. Susan Hanson (Minneapolis: University of Minnesota Press, 1993), xii, 17, 264–281; Maurice Blanchot, *L'entretien infini* (Paris: Gallimard, 1969), vii, 20, 394–418. See also Maurice Blanchot, "Do Not Forget," in *Political Writings, 1953–1993*, ed. and trans. Zakir Paul (New York: Fordham University Press, 2010), 127; Maurice Blanchot, "N'oubliez pas" (1988), in *Écrits politiques. Guerre d'Algérie, Mai 68, etc. (1958–1993)*, ed. Michel Surya (Paris: Lignes/Scheer, 2003), 170.

14. See Maurice Blanchot, *The Writing of the Disaster*, trans. Ann Smock (Lincoln: University of Nebraska Press, 1995), 93, 98, 101–104, 107; Maurice Blanchot, *L'écriture du désastre* (Paris: Gallimard, 1980), 146–154, 158–162, 166.

[In 1976, Malraux . . .]

Retitled for the present translation, this text was written as a response to a survey on intellectuals conducted by the journal *Lignes* and published originally in October 1997 (no. 32) under the title (given by the journal) "Les Intellectuels. Tentative d'une définition par eux-mêmes, enquête" (Intellectuals: An Attempt at Self-Definition—A Survey). For further details, see the Bibliographical Note at the end of this volume.

1. Charles de Gaulle (1890–1970).

2. The "Declaration on the Right to Insubordination in the Algerian War"—also known as the "Manifesto" or "Declaration of the 121"—was published in 1960. It was codrafted and signed by Blanchot, among others. See Maurice Blanchot, *Political Writings, 1953–1993*, ed. and trans. Zakir Paul (New York: Fordham University Press, 2010), 15–35; Maurice Blanchot, *Écrits politiques. Guerre d'Algérie, Mai 68, etc. (1958–1993)*, ed. Michel Surya (Paris: Lignes/Scheer, 2003), 27–42.

3. The Rassemblement pour le peuple français (RPF) was set up in 1947 by de Gaulle in order to implement the political program outlined in his two speeches given at Bayeux following the Liberation.

4. The Union pour la nouvelle république (UNR) was established in 1958 to support de Gaulle's policies after his return to power.

5. See Maurice Blanchot, "Intellectuals Under Scrutiny," in *The Blanchot Reader*, ed. and trans. Michael Holland (Oxford: Blackwell, 1995), 215; Maurice Blanchot, *Les intellectuels en question* (1984; Tours: Farrago, 2000), 29–30.

Interview with Pascal Possoz

This two-part interview was recorded on December 31, 2001 (Part I), and January 2, 2002 (Part II), on the premises of digital publisher Hors-Œil, in Montpellier, visited by Philippe Lacoue-Labarthe on a regular basis. At the time of the interview, Pascal Possoz, a gastroenterologist specializing in alcohol addiction, was preparing a doctorate in psychopathology, focusing on what he refers to as "self-Blanchot-analysis [*auto-blanchot-analyse*]" and proposing a clinical interpretation of certain Blanchotian motifs. The doctorate was the culmination of years of experience in the study and treatment of addiction, to which meditations on such notions as the *neutre*, *écart*, and *il* brought important contributions. Upon noticing the centrality of the dialogue between Blanchot and Lacoue-Labarthe around the question of the "primal scene" and anxious to offer a medical perspective on this question by paying particular attention to the possibility of relating the inscription of this primal scene to the construction of the psychical apparatus, Possoz took the initiative in interviewing Lacoue-Labarthe informally on what was at stake in the texts concerned and on how they came into being. As a result, the present interview was never meant to be published but served instead as a kind of memorandum to assist and guide Possoz in his doctoral work. The interview was rediscovered in 2011, just as *Agonie terminée, agonie interminable* was going to press; it is thus published (and translated) here for the first time.

1. Possoz is referring to Blanchot's text "A Primal Scene," which first appeared in 1976 in the review *Première Livraison*, edited by Lacoue-Labarthe and Mathieu Bénézet. See "Ending and Unending Agony," in the present volume.

2. On Mathieu Bénézet, see "Ending and Unending Agony," in the present volume.

3. See Maurice Blanchot, *The Writing of the Disaster*, trans. Ann Smock (Lincoln: University of Nebraska Press, 1995), 135; Maurice Blanchot, *L'écriture du désastre* (Paris: Gallimard, 1980), 205.

4. See Philippe Lacoue-Labarthe and Jean-Luc Nancy, *The Literary Absolute: The Theory of Literature in German Romanticism*, trans. Philip Barnard and Cheryl Lester (New York: SUNY Press, 1988); Philippe Lacoue-Labarthe and Jean-Luc Nancy, *L'absolu littéraire: Théorie de la littérature du romantisme allemande* (Paris: Le Seuil, 1978).

5. See Walter Benjamin, *Le concept de critique esthétique dans le romantisme allemand*, trans. Philippe Lacoue-Labarthe and Anne-Marie Lang (1986; Paris: Flammarion, 2008).

6. Founded in 1975 by Lacoue-Labarthe and Bénézet, the review published twelve issues altogether (six issues in 1975–1976, six in 1976–1977).

7. What later came to be known (for lack of a definitive title) as the *Revue Internationale* was an ambitious (but abortive) project elaborated from 1960 to 1964 by Maurice Blanchot, Dionys Mascolo, and a number of other contemporary intellectuals (among others, Louis-René des Forêts, Roland Barthes, Marguerite Duras, Italo Calvino, Pier Paolo Pasolini, Alberto Moravia, Hans Magnus Enzensberger, Uwe Johnson, and Günter Grass) in the wake of the "Declaration on the Right to Insubordination in the Algerian War." A full dossier on the *Revue* (including blueprints, drafts, preparatory texts, correspondence, etc.) was published in a special number of *Lignes* (1st series), 11 (September 1990).

8. An influential editor, Christian Bourgois (1933–2007) founded the eponymous publishing house in 1966. A number of Lacoue-Labarthe's works were published by Bourgois.

9. See Friedrich Hölderlin, *Antigone de Sophocle*, ed. and trans. Philippe Lacoue-Labarthe (Paris: Bourgois, 1998).

10. See Blanchot, *The Writing of the Disaster*, 72; Blanchot, *L'écriture du désastre*, 117.

11. See Mathieu Bénézet, *L'histoire de la peinture en trois volumes* (Paris: Gallimard, 1968).

12. See Mathieu Bénézet, *Dits et récits du mortel* (Paris: Flammarion, 1977).

13. See Mathieu Bénézet, Maurice Blanchot, Michel Deutsch, Emmanuel Hocquard, Philippe Lacoue-Labarthe, Roger Laporte, Jean-Luc Nancy, and Jean-Louis Schefer, *Misère de la littérature* (Paris: Bourgois, 1978).

14. See Mathieu Bénézet, Michel Deutsch, Emmanuel Hocquard, Philippe Lacoue-Labarthe, Jean-Luc Nancy, Bernard Noël, Alain Veinstein, and Franck Venaille, *"Haine de la poésie"* (Paris: Bourgois, 1979).

15. See Maurice Blanchot, *The Instant of My Death*, trans. Elizabeth Rottenberg (Stanford, Calif.: Stanford University Press, 2000), 3; Maurice Blanchot, *L'instant de ma mort* (1994; Paris: Gallimard, 2002), 9.

16. See *Les fins de l'homme: à partir du travail de Jacques Derrida* (Paris: Galilée, 1981).

17. See Serge Leclaire, *A Child Is Being Killed: On Primary Narcissism and the Death Drive*, trans. Marie-Claude Hays (Stanford, Calif.: Stanford University Press, 1998); Serge Leclaire, *On tue un enfant: un essai sur le narcissisme primaire et la pulsion de mort* (1975; Paris: Le Seuil, 1981).

18. See Donald Winnicott, "La crainte de l'effondrement," trans. Jeanine Kalmanovitch, *Nouvelle Revue de Psychanalyse* 11 (1975), special issue: "Figures du vide," 35–44.

19. See Nicolas Abraham and Maria Torok, *The Wolf Man's Magic Word: A Cryptonymy*, trans. Nicholas Rand (Minneapolis: University of Minnesota Press, 1986); Nicolas Abraham and Maria Torok, *Le verbier de l'homme aux loups, cryptonymie* (Paris: Flammarion, 1976).

20. See Jacques Derrida, "Fors: The Anglish Words of Nicolas Abraham and Maria Torok," trans. Barbara Johnson, in *The Wolf Man's Magic Word: A Cryptonymy*, xi–xlviii; Jacques Derrida, "Fors" (1976), in *Le verbier de l'homme aux loups, cryptonymie*, 7–73.

21. On the relationship between Colette Peignot (1903–1938), also known as Laure (Georges Bataille's lover), and Blanchot's *Death Sentence*, see Christophe Bident, *Maurice Blanchot. Partenaire invisible* (Seyssel: Champ Vallon, 1998), 291–294.

22. See "Dismay," in the present volume.

23. See "Dismay," in the present volume.

24. Blanchot, *The Writing of the Disaster*, 72; Blanchot, *L'écriture du désastre*, 117.

25. Blanchot, *The Writing of the Disaster*, 72; Blanchot, *L'écriture du désastre*, 117.

26. Philippe Lacoue-Labarthe is referring to the present volume.

27. The French jurist and psychoanalyst Pierre Legendre (b. 1930). For Legendre's discussion of narcissism, see his *Leçons IV. Les enfants du texte* (Paris: Fayard, 1992); and his *Leçons III. Dieu au miroir. Étude sur l'institution des images* (Paris: Fayard, 1993). A translation of an extract from the latter book has been published under the title "Introduction to the Theory of the Image: Narcissus and the Other in the Mirror," in *Law and the Unconscious: A Legendre Reader*, ed. and trans. Peter Goodrich (London: Macmillan, 1997), 211–254.

28. *Glace* is polysemous, meaning not just mirror but also ice or (plate) glass. Here as elsewhere in this interview, where the term "mirror" is not followed in square brackets by *glace*, the original French term translated is *miroir*.

29. Blanchot, *The Writing of the Disaster*, 72; Blanchot, *L'écriture du désastre*, 11.

30. See Bident, *Maurice Blanchot. Partenaire invisible*.

31. Maurice Blanchot, "Marx's Three Voices," trans. Tom Keenan, in *Friendship* (Stanford, Calif.: Stanford University Press, 1997), 98–100; Maurice Blanchot, "Les trois paroles de Marx" (1968), in *L'amitié* (Paris: Gallimard, 1971), 115–117.

32. See "Ending and Unending Agony," in the present volume.

33. Blanchot, *The Instant of My Death*, 5, 7; Blanchot, *L'instant de ma mort*, 11.

34. See the final line of "Dismay," in the present volume.

35. The Austrian psychoanalyst Theodor Reik (1888–1969). On Reik, see Philippe Lacoue-Labarthe, "The Echo of the Subject," in *Typography: Mimesis, Philosophy, Politics*, ed. Christopher Fynsk (Stanford, Calif.: Stanford University Press, 1998), 139–207; Philippe Lacoue-Labarthe, "L'écho du sujet," in *Le sujet de la philosophie. Typographies I* (Paris: Aubier-Flammarion, 1979), 217–303.

36. The French psychoanalyst Lucien Israël (1925–1996).

37. The Egyptian psychoanalyst Moustafa Safouan (b. 1921).

38. In English in the original.

39. The quality of the audio recording is particularly poor in this passage. Aristide Bianchi and Leonid Kharlamov transcribe it as: "Toute cette métaphorique ou liste médicale manipulée à cause des nazis a dû marquer les gens," that is: "All this metaphorical discourse, this medical language or list manipulated by the Nazis, must have left its mark on people." Listening to the recording myself, I think it is also possible, given the context, that Lacoue-Labarthe is saying: "Toute cette métaphorique—hygiéniste, médicale—manipulée à cause des nazis a dû marquer les gens," that is: "All this metaphorical language—of hygienics, of the medical—manipulated by the Nazis must have left its mark on people."

40. For Pascal Possoz's subsequent medical reading of Blanchot, see "La médecine en filigrane dans la vie et l'œuvre de Maurice Blanchot," in *Blanchot dans son siècle*, ed. Monique Antelme, Gisèle Berkman, Christophe Bident, et al. (Lyon: Parangon, 2009), 155–165.

41. See Blanchot, *The Writing of the Disaster*, 86–87; Blanchot, *L'écriture du désastre*, 137.

42. Philippe Lacoue-Labarthe is referring to Sontag's *Illness as Metaphor* (1978).

43. See Maurice Blanchot, "La rencontre avec le démon" (1955), in *La condition critique*, ed. Christophe Bident (Paris: Gallimard, 2010), 205–225.

44. G.W. F. Hegel, "The Ontological Proof, from the 1831 *Lectures on the Philosophy of Religion*," in *Lectures on the Proofs of the Existence of God*, trans. Peter C. Hodgson (Oxford: Oxford University Press, 2011), 192; G.W. F. Hegel, "Ausführung des ontologischen Beweises in den Vorlesungen über Religionsphilosophie vom Jahre 1831" (1831), *Vorlesungen über die Beweise Vom Dasein Gottes*, in *Werke in zwanzig Bänden* (Frankfurt a. M.: Suhrkamp, 1969), 17:534.

45. Blanchot, *The Writing of the Disaster*, 72; Blanchot, *L'écriture du désastre*, 117.

46. Maurice Blanchot, *The Step Not Beyond*, trans. Lycette Nelson (Albany, N.Y.: SUNY Press, 1992), 137; Maurice Blanchot, *Le pas au-delà* (Paris: Gallimard, 1973), 187.

47. Blanchot, *The Writing of the Disaster*, 135; Blanchot, *L'écriture du désastre*, 205.

48. Francis Pasche, "L'anti-narcissisme," *Revue Française de Psychanalyse* 29, no. 5–6 (1965): 503–518.

49. See "Ending and Unending Agony," in the present volume.

Dismay

This revised version of "Dismay" ["L'émoi"] was published in Philippe Lacoue-Labarthe, *Phrase* (Paris: Bourgois, 2000), 43–48. An earlier version of "Dismay" (dated "Summer 1976") appeared in *Digraphe* 18 (November 1978): 55–57.

1. "In the Lydian mode [*in der lydischen Tonart*]" refers to the musical mode assigned by Beethoven to the third movement of his String Quartet no. 15 in A minor, Op. 132. The full description reads: "A Convalescent's Holy Song of Thanksgiving to the Divinity, in the Lydian Mode [*Heiliger Dankgesang eines Genesenen an die Gottheit, in der lydischen Tonart*]." See also Lacoue-Labarthe, "Phrase XIV," in *Phrase*, 89–91.

Bibliographical Note

Texts Translated for This Volume

With the exception of "[In 1976, Malraux . . .]" and "Interview with Pascal Possoz," *Agonie terminée, agonie interminable. Sur Maurice Blanchot* (Paris: Galilée, 2011) is the source text for the present translation. Further bibliographical details on all texts translated for this volume are provided below.

"Prologue" ["Avant-propos," *Agonie terminée, agonie interminable*, 57–59]: originally entitled "Argumentaire" (Blurb) and written in 2003 as part of the book proposal for *Agonie terminée, agonie interminable* for publisher Galilée.

"Fidelities" ["Fidélités," *Agonie terminée, agonie interminable*, 63–90]: initially given as a conference paper at Cerisy-la-Salle in July 1997 and subsequently published in *L'animal autobiographique* (Paris: Galilée, 1999), 215–230. An English translation by Michael Syrotinski of a slightly shorter version of the final text appearing in *Agonie terminée, agonie interminable* was published in the *Oxford Literary Review* 22, no. 1 (July 2000), special number: "Disastrous Blanchot," 132–151.

"The Contestation of Death" ["La contestation de la mort," *Agonie terminée, agonie interminable*, 91–117]: initially given as a conference paper at the Annual Meeting of French Language and Literature Professors hosted by Matsuyama University (Japan) in October 1999 and first (partially) published in the *Magazine Littéraire* 424 (October 2003), special issue: "Maurice Blanchot," 58–60. An English translation by Philip Anderson of a shorter version of the final text appearing in *Agonie terminée, agonie interminable* was published in *The Power of Contestation: Perspectives on Maurice Blanchot*, ed. Kevin Hart and Geoffrey Hartman (Baltimore, Md.: Johns Hopkins University Press, 2004), 141–155.

"Birth Is Death" ["La naissance est la mort," *Agonie terminée, agonie interminable*, 119–125]: published originally in autumn 1994 in *Séquences* 27–28, a journal edited by the Théâtre national de Strasbourg, which at the time was staging a reading by Philippe Clévenot of Antonin Artaud's Vieux-Colombier lecture; republished under the same title in *Lignes* (new series) 22 (May 2007), special issue: "Philippe Lacoue-Labarthe," 242–247.

"The Agony of Religion" ["L'agonie de la religion," *Agonie terminée, agonie interminable*, 126–129]: initially written for a public reading organized at the Maison des écrivains in Paris to mark Maurice Blanchot's ninetieth birthday on September 22, 1997, and subsequently published in a special number (edited by Roger Laporte) of the *Revue des Sciences Humaines* 253 (January–March 1999), special issue: "Maurice Blanchot," 227–229.

"Ending and Unending Agony" ["Agonie terminée, agonie interminable," *Agonie terminée, agonie interminable*, 131–151]: initially given as a conference paper at Université de Paris-Diderot (Paris VII) in March 2003 and subsequently published in *Maurice Blanchot. Récits critiques*, ed. Christophe Bident and Pierre Vilar (Tours/Paris: Lignes/Scheer, 2003), 439–449.

"[In 1976, Malraux . . .]": written as a response to a survey on intellectuals conducted by the journal *Lignes* and published originally in issue 32 (October 1997) under the title (given by the journal) "Les Intellectuels. Tentative d'une définition par eux-mêmes, enquête" (Intellectuals: An Attempt at Self-Definition—A Survey); republished under the same title in *Lignes* (new series) 22 (May 2007), special issue: "Philippe Lacoue-Labarthe," 235–241. Retitled for the present translation.

"Interview with Pascal Possoz": two-part interview with Pascal Possoz recorded on December 31, 2001 (Part I), and January 2, 2002 (Part II), at the offices of digital publisher Hors-Œil in Montpellier, France. Heretofore unpublished.

"Dismay" ["L'émoi," *Agonie terminée, agonie interminable*, 153–159]: composed in August 1976 and first published in November 1978 in *Digraphe* 16 under the title "L'émoi"; republished in a revised version as "Phrase V (L'émoi)," in Philippe Lacoue-Labarthe, *Phrase* (Paris: Bourgois, 2000), 43–48.

English Translations Cited in This Volume

The following translations are listed alphabetically (and within each author by date of publication), with date of first publication of original text in brackets following title.

Abraham, Nicolas, and Maria Torok. *The Wolf Man's Magic Word: A Cryptonymy* [1976]. Trans. Nicholas Rand. Minneapolis: University of Minnesota Press, 1986.

Bataille, Georges. *Inner Experience* [1943]. Trans. Leslie Boldt. Albany, N.Y.: SUNY Press, 1988.

———. "Hegel, Death, and Sacrifice" [1955]. Trans. Jonathan Strauss. *Yale French Studies* 78 (1990): 9–28.

———. *Manet* [1955]. Trans. Austryn Wainhouse and James Emmons. London: Macmillan, 1983.

Benjamin, Walter. "On the Concept of History" [1940]. In *Selected Writings*, trans. Edmund Jephcott et al., ed. Howard Eiland and Michael W. Jennings, 4:389–400. Cambridge, Mass.: Harvard University Press, 2003.

Blanchot, Maurice. *Faux pas* [1943]. Trans. Charlotte Mandell. Stanford, Calif.: Stanford University Press, 2001.

———. "Kafka and the Work's Demand" [1952]. In *The Space of Literature*, trans. Ann Smock, 57–84. Lincoln: University of Nebraska Press, 1982.

———. *The Space of Literature* [1955]. Trans. Ann Smock. Lincoln: University of Nebraska Press, 1982.

———. "The Very Last Word" [1968]. In *Friendship*, trans. Elizabeth Rottenberg, 265–288. Stanford, Calif.: Stanford University Press, 1997.

———. "Marx's Three Voices" [1968]. In *Friendship*, trans. Tom Keenan, 98–100. Stanford, Calif.: Stanford University Press, 1997.

———. *The Infinite Conversation* [1969]. Trans. Susan Hanson. Minneapolis: University of Minnesota Press, 1993.
———. "The Last to Speak" [1972]. In *A Voice from Elsewhere*, trans. Charlotte Mandell, 53–93. Albany, N.Y.: SUNY Press, 2007.
———. *The Step Not Beyond* [1973]. Trans. Lycette Nelson. Albany, N.Y.: SUNY Press, 1992.
———. *The Writing of the Disaster* [1980]. Trans. Ann Smock. Lincoln: University of Nebraska Press, 1995.
———. *The Unavowable Community* [1983]. Trans. Pierre Joris. Barrytown, N.Y.: Station Hill, 1988.
———. "Intellectuals Under Scrutiny" [1984]. In *The Blanchot Reader*, ed. and trans. Michael Holland, 206–227. London: Blackwell, 1995.
———. "[Thinking the Apocalypse]" [1988]. In *Political Writings, 1953–1993*, ed. and trans. Zakir Paul, 119–123. New York: Fordham University Press, 2010.
———. "Do Not Forget" [1988]. In *Political Writings, 1953–1993*, ed. and trans. Zakir Paul, 124–129. New York: Fordham University Press, 2010.
———. "For Friendship" [1993]. In *Political Writings, 1953–1993*, ed. and trans. Zakir Paul, 134–143. New York: Fordham University Press, 2010.
———. *The Instant of My Death* [1994]. Trans. Elizabeth Rottenberg. Stanford, Calif.: Stanford University Press, 2000.
———. *Political Writings, 1953–1993* [2003; 2008]. Ed. and trans. Zakir Paul. New York: Fordham University Press, 2010.
Borges, Jorge Luis, "The Secret Miracle" [1943]. In *Fictions*, trans. Andrew Hurley, 124–131. London: Penguin, 2000.
Celan, Paul. "The Meridian" [1960]. In *Selected Poems and Prose of Paul Celan*, trans. John Felstiner, 401–414. New York: Norton, 2001.
———. "Ash-aureole" [1964]. In *Selected Poems and Prose of Paul Celan*, trans. John Felstiner, 260–261. New York: Norton, 2001.
Derrida, Jacques. "Fors: The Anglish Words of Nicolas Abraham and Maria Torok" [1976]. Trans. Barbara Johnson. In *The Wolf Man's Magic Word: A Cryptonymy*, trans. Nicholas Rand, xi–xlviii. Minneapolis: University of Minnesota Press, 1986.
———. "Desistance" [1989]. In *Typography: Mimesis, Philosophy, Politics* [1989], ed. and trans. Christopher Fynsk, 1–42. Stanford, Calif.: Stanford University Press, 1998.
———. *Demeure: Fiction and Testimony* [1998]. Trans. Elizabeth Rottenberg. Stanford, Calif.: Stanford University Press, 2000.
Freud, Sigmund. "On Narcissism: An Introduction" [1914]. In *The Standard Edition of the Complete Psychological Works of Sigmund Freud*, ed. James Strachey, 14:73–102. London: Hogarth, 1957.
———. "From the History of an Infantile Neurosis" [1918]. In *The Standard Edition of the Complete Psychological Works of Sigmund Freud*, ed. James Strachey, 17:7–122. London: Hogarth, 1955.
———. "Analysis Terminable and Interminable" [1937]. In *The Standard Edition of the Complete Psychological Works of Sigmund Freud*, ed. James Strachey, 23:211–253. London: Vintage, 2001.

Hegel, G.W. F. *Natural Law* [1802–1803]. Trans. T. M. Knox. Philadelphia: University of Pennsylvania Press, 1975.

———. *Phenomenology of Spirit* [1807]. Trans. A.V. Miller. Oxford: Clarendon, 1977.

———. "The Ontological Proof, from the 1831 *Lectures on the Philosophy of Religion*" [1831]. In *Lectures on the Proofs of the Existence of God*, trans. Peter C. Hodgson, 187–193. Oxford: Oxford University Press, 2011.

Heidegger, Martin. *Off the Beaten Track* [1950]. Ed. and trans. Julian Young and Kenneth Haynes. Cambridge: Cambridge University Press, 2002.

———. *Identity and Difference* [1957]. Trans. Joan Stambaugh. Chicago: University of Chicago Press, 1969.

Hölderlin, Friedrich. Letter to his brother, January 1, 1799. In *Essays and Letters on Theory*, trans. Thomas Pfau, 136–140. Albany, N.Y.: SUNY Press, 1988.

———. "Remarks on *Antigone*" [1804]. In *Essays and Letters on Theory*, trans. Thomas Pfau, 109–116. Albany, N.Y.: SUNY Press, 1988.

———. "Patmos" [1808]. In *Poems and Fragments*, bilingual ed., trans. Michael Hamburger, 550–565. London: Anvil, 2004.

———. "In lovely blueness . . ." [1823]. In *Poems and Fragments*, bilingual ed., trans. Michael Hamburger, 788–793. London: Anvil, 2004.

Kant, Immanuel. *Critique of Pure Reason* [1781; 1787]. Ed. and trans. Paul Guyer and Allen W. Wood. Cambridge: Cambridge University Press, 1998.

Lacan, Jacques. *Anxiety: The Seminar of Jacques Lacan, Book X* [1982]. Ed. Jacques-Alain Miller, trans. A. R. Price. Cambridge, UK: Polity, 2014.

———. *The Ethics of Psychoanalysis, 1959–1960: The Seminar of Jacques Lacan, Book VII* [1986]. Ed. Jacques-Alain Miller, trans. Dennis Porter. London: Routledge, 2008.

Lacoue-Labarthe, Philippe. "The Fable (Literature and Philosophy)" [1970]. In *The Subject of Philosophy*, ed. Thomas Trezise, trans. Hugh J. Silverman, 1–13. Minneapolis: University of Minnesota Press, 1993.

———. "Apocryphal Nietzsche" [1973]. In *The Subject of Philosophy*, ed. Thomas Trezise, trans. Timothy D. Bent, 32–56. Minneapolis: University of Minnesota Press, 1993.

———. "Obliteration" [1973]. In *The Subject of Philosophy*, ed. and trans. Thomas Trezise, 57–98. Minneapolis: University of Minnesota Press, 1993.

———. "Typography" [1975]. In *Typography: Mimesis, Philosophy, Politics* [1989], ed. Christopher Fynsk, trans. Eduardo Cadava, 43–138. Stanford, Calif.: Stanford University Press, 1998.

———. "The Echo of the Subject" [1975–1976]. In *Typography: Mimesis, Philosophy, Politics* [1989], ed. Christopher Fynsk, trans. Barbara Harlow, 139–207. Stanford, Calif.: Stanford University Press, 1998.

———. "The Caesura of the Speculative" [1978]. In *Typography: Mimesis, Philosophy, Politics* [1989], ed. Christopher Fynsk, trans. Robert Eisenhauer, 208–235. Stanford, Calif.: Stanford University Press, 1998.

———. "In the Name of . . ." [1980]. In Philippe Lacoue-Labarthe and Jean-Luc Nancy, *Retreating the Political*, ed. and trans. Simon Sparks, 55–78. London: Routledge, 1997.

———. "Transcendence Ends in Politics" [1981]. In *Typography: Mimesis, Philosophy,*

Politics [1989], ed. Christopher Fynsk, trans. Peter Caws, 267–300. Stanford, Calif.: Stanford University Press, 1998.

———. *Poetry as Experience* [1986]. Trans. Andrea Tarnowski. Stanford, Calif.: Stanford University Press, 1999.

———. *Heidegger, Art, and Politics: The Fiction of the Political* [1987]. Trans. Chris Turner. Oxford: Blackwell, 1990.

———. "Il faut" [1992]. In *Heidegger and the Politics of Poetry*, trans. Jeff Fort, 38–59. Urbana: University of Illinois Press, 2007.

Lacoue-Labarthe, Philippe, and Jean-Luc Nancy. *The Literary Absolute: The Theory of Literature in German Romanticism* [1978]. Trans. Philip Barnard and Cheryl Lester. Albany, N.Y.: SUNY Press, 1988.

———. "The Jewish People Do Not Dream" [1981], part 1 ("The Unconscious Is Destructured Like an Affect") and 2 ("From Where Is Psychoanalysis Possible?"). Trans. Brian Holmes. *Stanford Literature Review* 6, no. 2 (Fall 1989): 191–209; 8, no. 1–2 (Spring–Fall 1991): 39–55.

———. "Noli me frangere" [1982]. In Jean-Luc Nancy, *The Birth to Presence*, trans. Brian Holmes et al., 266–278. Stanford, Calif.: Stanford University Press, 1993.

———. "The Nazi Myth" [1991]. Trans. Brian Holmes. *Critical Inquiry* 16, no. 2 (Winter 1990): 291–312.

Leclaire, Serge. *A Child Is Being Killed: On Primary Narcissism and the Death Drive* [1975]. Trans. Marie-Claude Hays. Stanford, Calif.: Stanford University Press, 1998.

Legendre, Pierre. "Introduction to the Theory of the Image: Narcissus and the Other in the Mirror." In *Law and the Unconscious: A Legendre Reader*, ed. and trans. Peter Goodrich, 211–254. London: Macmillan, 1997. Translation of an extract from *Leçons III. Dieu au miroir. Étude sur l'institution des images* (Paris: Fayard, 1993).

Lyotard, Jean-François. "Tomb of the Intellectual" [1983]. In *Political Writings*, trans. Bill Readings and Kevin Paul Geiman, 3–7. London: UCL Press, 1993.

Mallarmé, Stéphane. Letter to Henri Cazalis, May 14, 1867. In *Selected Letters of Stéphane Mallarmé*, trans. Rosemary Lloyd, 74–76. Chicago: University of Chicago Press, 1988.

——— Letter to Eugène Lefébure, May 27, 1867. In *Selected Letters of Stéphane Mallarmé*, trans. Rosemary Lloyd, 76–81. Chicago. University of Chicago Press, 1988.

———. "Arthur Rimbaud" [1896]. In *Divagations*, trans. Barbara Johnson, 64–72. Cambridge, Mass.: Harvard University Press, 2007.

———. "Verlaine's Tomb" [1897]. In *Sonnets*, trans. David Scott, 92–93. Exeter: Shearsman, 2008.

Malraux, André. *The Walnut Trees of Altenburg* [1943; 1948]. Trans. A.W. Fielding. Chicago: University of Chicago Press, 1992.

———. *Antimemoirs* [1967]. Trans. Terence Kilmartin. London: Hamish Hamilton, 1968.

Mann, Thomas. "Freud and the Future" [1936]. In *Essays of Three Decades*, trans. H.T. Lowe-Porter, 411–428. London: Secker & Warburg, 1947.

Montaigne, Michel de. "On Practice" [1580]. In *Essays*, trans. M.A. Screech, 416–427. London: Penguin, 2003.

Nietzsche, Friedrich. *Ecce Homo* [1889]. In *The Anti-Christ, Ecce Homo, Twilight of the Idols, and Other Writings*, ed. Aaron Ridley, trans. Judith Norman, 69–151. Cambridge: Cambridge University Press, 2005.

Pascal, Blaise. "The Memorial" [1670]. In *Pensées and Other Writings*, trans. Honor Levi, 178. Oxford: Oxford University Press, 1995.

Plato. *Phaedo*. Trans. David Gallop. Oxford: Oxford University Press, 2009.

———. *The Republic*. Trans. Robin Waterfield. Oxford: Oxford University Press, 2008.

Rousseau, Jean-Jacques. *Reveries of the Solitary Walker* [1782]. Trans. Russell Goulbourne. Oxford: Oxford University Press, 2011.

———. *The Confessions* [1782–1789]. Trans. J. M. Cohen. London: Penguin, 1953.

Surya, Michel. *Georges Bataille: An Intellectual Biography* [1992]. Trans. Krzysztof Fijalkowski and Michael Richardson. London: Verso, 2009.

Vidal-Naquet, Pierre. *The Black Hunter* [1981]. Trans. Andrew Szegedy-Maszak. Baltimore, Md.: Johns Hopkins University Press, 1986.

Index of Names

Sara Guyer and Brian McGrath, series editors

Sara Guyer, *Reading with John Clare: Biopoetics, Sovereignty, Romanticism.*

Philippe Lacoue-Labarthe, *Ending and Unending Agony: On Maurice Blanchot*. Translated by Hannes Opelz.